SECOND EDITION

S0-AAZ-852

Leadership Strategies
for
SAFE
SCHOOLS

For my models of constructive conflict resolution

For my parents, Shirley and Joseph, the diplomat and the peacemaker
For my brother, Raymond, the problem solver
For my husband, Michael, the collaborator

SECOND EDITION

Leadership Strategies for SAFE SCHOOLS

Elizabeth A. Barton

CORWIN
A SAGE Company

For information:

Corwin
A SAGE Company
2455 Teller Road
Thousand Oaks, California 91320
(800) 233-9936
Fax: (800) 417-2466
www.corwinpress.com

SAGE Ltd.
1 Oliver's Yard
55 City Road
London EC1Y 1SP
United Kingdom

SAGE India Pvt. Ltd.
B 1/I 1 Mohan Cooperative
   Industrial Area
Mathura Road, New Delhi 110 044
India

SAGE Asia-Pacific Pte. Ltd.
33 Pekin Street #02-01
Far East Square
Singapore 048763

Printed in the United States of America.

Library of Congress Cataloging-in-Publication Data

Barton, Elizabeth A.
Leadership strategies for safe schools / Elizabeth A. Barton. — 2nd ed.
       p. cm.
Includes bibliographical references and index.
ISBN 978-1-4129-5567-6 (cloth)
ISBN 978-1-4129-5568-3 (pbk.)

   1. Schools—United States—Security measures—Handbooks, manuals, etc. 2. School violence—United States—Prevention—Handbooks, manuals, etc. 3. School management and organization—United States—Handbooks, manuals, etc. 4. Conflict management—Handbooks, manuals, etc. I. Title.

LB2866.B37 2009
371.7'820973—dc22   2008049664

This book is printed on acid-free paper.

09   10   11   12   13   10 9 8 7 6 5 4 3 2 1

Acquisitions Editor:	Cathy Hernandez
Editorial Assistant:	Sarah Bartlett
Production Editor:	Libby Larson
Copy Editor:	Paula L. Fleming
Typesetter:	C&M Digitals (P) Ltd.
Proofreader:	Wendy Jo Dymond
Indexer:	Jean Casalegno
Cover Designer:	Michael Dubowe

Contents

Acknowledgments

Corwin gratefully acknowledges the contributions of the following reviewers:

Kathy Bohan
Assistant Professor of Educational Psychology
Northern Arizona University
Sedona, AZ

Jeff Daniels
Assistant Professor of Counseling & Educational Psychology
Indiana University
Bloomington, IN

Patti Kinney
Principal
Talent Middle School
Ashland, OR

Richard Meyer
Principal
Holdrege High School
Holdrege, NE

Elizabeth Neale
Principal
Silvio O. Conte Community School
Pittsfield, MA

Nina Orellana
Third-Grade Teacher
Tenderloin Community School
San Francisco, CA

Ernie Rambo
Teacher, Electives 7–8
Walter Johnson Jr. High School
Las Vegas, NV

About the Author

 **Elizabeth A. Barton,** PhD, is associate director of the Center for Peace and Conflict Studies and Assistant Professor (Research) at Wayne State University in Detroit, Michigan. As a developmental psychologist specializing in socio-emotional development, she has served as a national consultant on school-based violence for over a decade. Barton oversees comprehensive violence prevention programming in 17 public schools and serves as the academic adviser to Community Engagement@Wayne, a center dedicated to engaging students in service learning experiences in Detroit.

Elizabeth recently received a U.S. Department of Education grant to study violence exposure on learning in a longitudinal sample of urban youth and is currently conducting a statewide assessment in Michigan of organizational readiness for youth violence prevention programs. Barton is the author of numerous publications, including *Bullying Prevention: Tips and Strategies for School Leaders and Classroom Teachers* and *Creating Harmony in the Classroom: Building Safe and Inclusive Classrooms for Special Populations.* She is an Urban Health Initiative Fellow, a national program of the Robert Wood Johnson Foundation. She earned her PhD and MA at Wayne State University and BS at the University of Michigan.

Introduction

THE PROBLEM OF SCHOOL SAFETY

Over the past two decades, U.S. educational institutions have experienced a pattern of school violence that has shattered the sense of security that students, their families, educators, and community members once held about school facilities and the schooling process. Communities in Colorado, Arkansas, Pennsylvania, and Virginia have been forever changed due to violence in the schools, and these are merely a representative sample of the incidents occurring in schools across America. Deadly occurrences are becoming more prevalent in schools in suburban and rural communities, crossing traditional socioeconomic, racial, and ethnic boundaries.

Yet, schools and classrooms across the country are relatively safe (Kingery & Walker, 2002). Children are more likely to be involved in a violent crime at home and in their neighborhoods than in school. The total number of students killed and wounded on school grounds in the 1990s was close in number to those in earlier decades (National Center on Education Statistics, 2007). Why then are schools now perceived as unsafe?

Indeed, the lack of perceived safety has much to do with the magnitude and impact of these tragedies. Characteristics of recent school shootings have been different due to the following:

- The number of killed and wounded per episode or tragedy
- The number and type of weapons used by the perpetrators
- The randomness by which victims were selected as targets
- The careful planning and conspiratorial nature of these school shootings
- The copycat nature of many of the shootings
- The use of school shootings as an instrument for settling scores for grievances, real or imagined

Nationally, school shootings have become matters of domestic terrorism. Following the 9/11 national tragedy, the federal government moved elements of the Office of Safe and Drug-Free Schools to the new Office of Homeland Security. Taking their cues from the federal government, school leaders across the country reacted by implementing school safety strategies that immediately impacted the quality of the school environment. Reactive, product-based strategies to create safe schools flooded the nation. Metal detectors, surveillance equipment, communication systems, and services of security guards were purchased. But do these measures improve safety on school campuses?

Students say surveillance cameras help to identify perpetrators only after the fact, and they report that metal detectors encourage some students to bring weapons to school to see if they can get away with them. Security guards are often afraid of violent students and do not have authority to arrest or detain students. Most significant is that reactive measures do not address the underlying causes and contributors to violence on campus.

Students need to perceive that their school is "safe"; in other words, the school is free environmentally and socially of any potential harm and danger. Clearly, learning cannot occur when safety issues distract students. Students often report fear of walking in certain areas of the school building, of using the restroom alone, even of the threat of violence on the school buses that take them to and from school. In 2005, approximately 6 percent of students ages 12 to 18 reported that they were afraid of attack or harm at school, and 5 percent reported that they were afraid of attack or harm away from school. Nine percent of Black students and 10 percent of Hispanic students reported that they were afraid of being attacked at school (including on the way to and from school), compared with 4 percent of White students (controlling for school location).

Hence, school leaders are becoming increasingly responsible for a new "primary" responsibility of creating safer schools for students concurrently with a "secondary" mission of developing and helping students realize cognitive goals.

The goals of creating safer schools and improving students' cognitive skills can be linked through the concept of conflict. Rather than veiwing conflict in negative terms as a result of the increase in violence in schools, school leaders should identify conflict as an opportunity for social and cognitive growth. Teaching constructive methods of conflict resolution provides school leaders with a student-driven mechanism for creating safer schools while improving students' problem-solving abilities. This student-driven, proactive approach to school safety is a critical component in creating quality learning environments while improving students' cognitive capabilities. Research indicates that children with more sophisticated problem-solving abilities demonstrate greater academic competence and greater ability to recover from such at-risk variables as low self-worth and poor peer relations (Johnson & Johnson, 1993). Students involved in conflict resolution programming excel in cooperative learning, demonstrating greater perspective-taking skills and greater sensitivity toward student differences. In addition, teachers report fewer discipline problems with students exposed to constructive conflict resolution education.

THE NEED FOR A PROACTIVE APPROACH TO SCHOOL SAFETY

Through a proactive approach to school safety issues involving constructive conflict resolution education, students develop both academically and socially. Regrettably, since 1990, school leaders have increasingly adopted a reactive approach rather than a proactive approach by installing metal detectors, surveillance equipment, and hiring additional guards. Each day, students in middle and senior high schools stand in line to enter the school through machines guarded by hired security personnel. In reality, acts of violence continue in these schools but out of sight of the video cameras and without the use of metal weapons.

The school safety strategy of teaching conflict resolution methods in public schools began in the 1970s, when parents and educators faced a growing concern regarding violence among children. The first recognized conflict resolution education program was the Children's Project for Friends, a Quaker project that taught nonviolence in New York City's public schools. A number of organizations evolved from the project, including the Children's Creative Response to Conflict, Educators for Social Responsibilities, and the Center for Peace and Conflict Studies at Wayne State University.

Today, conflict resolution education programs are widespread. T. Jones (2004) estimates that approximately 15,000 to 20,000 of the nation's 85,000 public schools engage in some form of conflict resolution education. Across the country, school administrators and staff teach students violence prevention techniques and general school safety procedures through programs such as curriculum integration, peer mediation training, and school building safety education. Through curriculum integration and peer mediation programs, students also learn life skills such as conflict resolution, communication, cooperation, character, and anger management, while school safety programs teach students how to avoid dangerous situations, places, and people.

STRATEGIES FOR CREATING SAFE SCHOOLS

Leadership Strategies for Safe Schools provides guidance to school leaders and school change agents primarily on proactive, preventive methods of building safe schools through student education. School leaders interested in developing and implementing new student-driven conflict resolution education programs will find the recommendations particularly beneficial. However, school leaders who wish to augment a current program, such as a peer mediation program, with a schoolwide character education program or who wish to improve community involvement with the school programming will also benefit from the book. Finally, the book also assists school leaders in reviewing their current educational programs for purposes of evaluation and adoption of alternative programming.

The text assists with the assessment, development, implementation, evaluation, and revision of school safety plans. Perhaps most importantly, *Leadership Strategies for Safe Schools* emphasizes that conflict is a natural, human occurrence and its successful, constructive resolution leads to more productive social relationships, stronger problem-solving skills (academic competence), and, in turn, safer schools. The somewhat new connection between community involvement and safe schools is based on the acceptance by educational leaders, criminal justice experts, and others of more current research in the field.

Although it emphasizes a proactive approach, the text does not ignore the relevance of other safe school initiatives, such as environmental changes that may be necessary in school safety planning. The book describes these initiatives as possible charges of the school safety team and its assessment of school safety needs.

The book's recommendations for practical safe school strategies are not intended to serve as sole practices in ensuring every school and classroom a safe school year.

Please note that school leaders interested in developing safer schools should assess the readiness and capacity of the school to implement institutional changes. Successful systemic change around school safety includes involvement by teachers and school administrators in initiating and sustaining program support, flexibility and problem-solving ability, administrative and staff stability, and philosophical compatibility with change efforts (Gottfredson & Gottfredson, 2002; Mihalic, 2004).

In addition, both fiscal resources and the availability and willingness of staff members to implement new safety strategies affect school safety program success. School leaders should take time to acknowledge how these organizational features may ultimately affect the success of the school safety initiatives (Elliot & Mihalic, 2004).

ORGANIZATION OF THE BOOK

Leadership Strategies for Safe Schools provides school leaders with practical strategies and information to develop, implement, and sustain safe school strategies in classrooms and schools. It provides a foundation for understanding the importance of constructive conflict resolution education, demonstrates direct applications and tools for successful programs, and suggests support for resources necessary to run effective programs.

Chapter 1: Creating a Safe School outlines current No Child Left Behind (NCLB) legislation and its impact on the definition of a safe school. Indicators of safe schools are discussed.

Chapter 2: Setting the Foundation describes methods building a safety school team and determining school safety needs. Successful school safety programs must meet the needs of the student climate, which varies greatly among schools. Efforts to prevent and mitigate violence must be targeted to the specific needs and assets of schools and school districts (Mihalic & Aultman-Bettridge, 2004). With the growing trend of violence in schools, school leaders are becoming increasingly aware of the importance of measuring issues related to school safety and their own role in assessment tool development, implementation, and evaluation.

Chapter 3: Positioning Character Development in School Curricula discusses the current trends in character education, or student responsibility, in school curricula. This chapter establishes the connection between character education and conflict resolution education and provides practical applications for both educational goals and objectives.

Chapter 4: Implementing Conflict Resolution Education describes the common goals and objectives for conflict resolution programming and demonstrates how school leaders can implement these goals within current curricula. The chapter discusses current programs available to educators and highlights how to refit current educational standards to include conflict resolution and violence prevention programming.

Chapter 5: Peer Mediation Programming serves as a practical overview of peer mediation, a common violence prevention technique.

Chapter 6: Integrating Diversity Into Conflict Resolution Education Programs describes the connection between student diversity and conflict in schools. Integrating the principles of diversity education with conflict resolution education is integral to the effectiveness of all school programming, even in nondiverse student populations.

Chapter 7: Evaluating School Safety Programs details methods school leaders can use to measure the effectiveness of school safety programs and ensure the stability of school safety in the future.

WHAT'S NEW IN THE SECOND EDITION

The second edition of *Leadership Strategies for Safe Schools* contains a number of modifications that will better assist school leaders with assessing, developing, implementing, and evaluating proactive strategies for safe schools. Case studies, scenarios, and classroom activities have been added throughout the book to provide real-life examples of the concepts and strategies presented. Research has been updated throughout, with a particular emphasis on marginalized populations, including lesbian, gay, bisexual, and transgender/transsexual (LGBT) adolescents.

1

Creating a Safe School

Caseville School has had two incidents of violence in the past year. In accordance with zero-tolerance policies, the violent acts resulted in the expulsion of three students, who were charged for assault with weapons. Guards patrol the halls, entrances have metal detectors, and all incidents of violence are reported to the police. Is this a safe school?

Jackson School has had no reported incidents of violence in the past year. Approximately 30 percent of the student population will not be returning to the school for the new school year. Almost all of the nonreturning students enrolled in the school one year ago, following a newly developed school-of-choice program. Is this a safe school?

Lenox School is located in a peaceful rural community in the Midwest. The school has no reported acts of violence in the past year. Truancy rates are high, with up to 27 percent of the student population absent on a regular basis. Six students have committed suicide in the past year. Is this a safe school?

DEFINING A SAFE SCHOOL

Defining a safe school is difficult. Is a safe school one in which guards patrol the halls and surveillance equipment is posted at school entrances? As in the example of Caseville, the school has had few incidents of violence, yet these acts involved weapons. Zero-tolerance policies (enforced through the Gun-Free Schools Act of 1994) resulted in several students being expelled from the school.

Alternatively, is a safe school one in which violence hasn't occurred but students from outside of the school district do not feel safe or included? Retention concerns in schools-of-choice, highlighted in the Jackson case, may indicate that policies, procedures, and/or a school culture is marginalizing students. Ostracized, excluded, or targeted students may become victims or perpetrators of crimes in an unwelcoming school.

Or is a safe school one that is peaceful but has seen students engage in self-violence, such as Lenox? In this example, students are reflecting an environment with few explicit signs of violence. Rather, the high truancy rate and suicide statistics may point to implicit acts of violence in the school consistent with the rampant expression of bullying behaviors.

Can schools be identified by the mutually exclusive categories of *safe* or *unsafe*? Or are schools better positioned to be viewed using a *continuum* from safe to unsafe, given specific student and school characteristics. For instance, is the safety of a school best operationalized by the number of disciplinary offenses? Perceptions of safety on campus as reported by parents/guardians, students, faculty? Or is safety more accurately based on the academic success of its students?

Most school leaders would agree that a safe school must be more than a school without fights, knifings, and shootings. But what characteristics clearly define a safe school and, thus, differentiate it from an unsafe school?

Indicators of a Safe School

A safe school is a place where the business of education can be conducted in a welcoming environment free of intimidation, violence, and fear. Such a setting provides an educational climate that fosters a spirit of acceptance and care for every child. It is a place free of bullying where behavior expectations are clearly communicated, consistently enforced, and fairly applied.

—Ronald D. Stephens, executive director, National
School Safety Center (Mabie, 2003, "What Is a Safe School?")

Research on understanding and describing indicators of a safe school shows that safe schools possess the following characteristics:

- A team-developed **safe school plan** and implementation strategy
- A committed administration that allocates **resources** for implementing the safe school plan
- Teaching and support staff with **positive relationships** and effective methods of **communicating** with their students, adults in the building, and parents/guardians
- **Comprehensive student programming** to reduce violent and aggressive behaviors (e.g. peer mediation, problem solving)

- Programming and policies that address **implicit forms** of violence and aggression between and among students. Implicit forms include bullying and biased-based violence.
- **Clean learning environments** both inside and adjacent to the building
- Commitment to a culture of learning with **high academic standards** and civil and respectful classrooms
- **Partnerships with the community**, including the business community surrounding the school

Safe schools have **school safety plans** that are user-friendly and up-to-date and whose contents are communicated to and practiced by school staff through tabletop exercises. In Chapter 2, the school safety plan, safety team composition, and development of implementation strategies will be explored. School safety plans, once the sole strategy for establishing and maintaining safety priorities, are, in some districts, just dust-covered documents. On the other hand, well-planned and executed safety plans create a learning environment that is both physically and emotionally safe for students, staff, and administrators.

School leaders must allocate **resources** for prevention and intervention strategies designed to create safe schools. School leaders who allocate resources are demonstrating to faculty, students, and parents/guardians that a safe school is a priority, thus immediately impacting the school culture in a constructive manner. In addition to directing funds toward programming, administrators must find ways to motivate teachers who support safe learning environments. Professional development, public recognition, course release time, and other forms of incentives do not always require money.

Grant support through the Safe and Drug-Free Schools and Communities programs and Safe Schools/Healthy Students programs are only two examples of funding available for safe schools initiatives. Private, local foundations may also be interested in providing support for specific prevention and intervention strategies. In addition, many schools are reaching out to the business community for both cash donations and person power support.

Safe schools have teaching and support staff with **positive relationships** and effective methods of **communicating** with their students, adults in the building, and parents/guardians. Werner and Smith's (1989) study, covering more than 40 years, finds that, among the most frequently encountered positive role models in the lives of resilient children, outside of the family circle, were favorite teachers. Such teachers were not just instructors for academic skills but also confidants and positive models for personal identification. Furthermore, Noddings (1988) finds that a caring relationship with a teacher gives students motivation to succeed.

Comprehensive **conflict resolution education** and violence prevention programming encourages students to share responsibility for creating a safe, secure school environment (Stomfay-Stitz, 1994). Strategies for implementing programming are located in Chapters 4 and 5 of this book. Students who are exposed to school-based social skills training programs that emphasize trust, respect, and nonviolent alternatives are less likely to engage frequently in violence and other problem behaviors. In addition to knowledge and behavioral improvements, students exposed to programming are more resilient to other school-based risk factors.

Bullying, punking, and biased-based violence and exclusion are addressed in safe schools through programming and policies and procedures. *Punking* is a practice of verbal and physical violence, humiliation, and shaming usually done in public by males to other males. Punking terminology and behaviors are usually interchangeable with bullying terminology and behaviors. Both practices are purposeful strategies used by many boys to affirm masculinity norms of toughness, strength, dominance, and control (Phillips, 2007).

Safe schools are **clean**. Students who learn in school buildings that are clean, well cared for, and supervised perceive these places as safe. Schools with clear perimeters that are supervised and controlled are more conducive to student learning than schools with ill-defined and unsupervised access points.

Schools with a commitment to a culture of learning, that possess **high academic standards**, and that demand civil and respectful classrooms are safe. Research indicates that schools that establish high expectations for all youth—and give them the support necessary to achieve them—have high rates of academic success. They also have lower rates of problem behaviors, such as dropping out, drug abuse, teen pregnancy, and delinquency, than other schools (Rutter, Maughan, Mortimore, Ouston, & Smith, 1979).

The Council for Corporate & School Partnerships, established in March 2001, serves as a forum for the exchange of information, expertise, and ideas to ensure that partnerships between businesses and schools achieve their full potential for meeting key educational objectives. At the end of 2003, the Council announced the National School and Business Partnerships Award to recognize school-business partnerships that improve the academic, social, or physical well-being of students. The Council publishes *The How-To Guide for School-Business Partnerships*, a road map to help schools and businesses successfully create, implement, sustain, and evaluate school-business partnerships.

Schools must be able to depend on the surrounding **community** to assist with school safety issues, because communities benefit from safe schools and are negatively affected by unsafe schools. A healthier school can do much for creating and maintaining healthier social and economic infrastructures in the surrounding communities. Partnerships with local businesses can also be extremely important in school safety programs. Safe schools provide local businesses with well-educated customers, a well-trained potential workforce, and quality education for children of their employees. Businesses can provide schools with financial assistance in maintaining school safety programs in addition to supplying a strong volunteer base for implementing school safety initiatives, such as patrolling school campuses before and after school and maintaining clean classroom and school environments.

Some of the most successful forms of business partnerships involve the following activities:

- Adopt-a-school program: Business owners and employees focus efforts on a particular school in the community. Activities include allowing employees time off to volunteer at the schools for mentoring, tutoring, job fair days, and other school activities.
- "Peacemaker of the Week" sponsorship: School staff select a student who demonstrates outstanding achievement in the area of school safety. The sponsoring business recognizes this student, perhaps by hanging the student's picture in the business and, if the business is a store, offering the student a gift of store merchandise.
- Job exposure and training for secondary students: Businesses offer students training in school safety-related topics, such as team building and interpersonal skills.
- Employment opportunities for students: Businesses that offer employment or internship opportunities are very beneficial to building safer schools. Students receive important work experience, and afterschool employment might help address the high rate of juvenile criminal activity that occurs between 3:00 and 4:00 PM (Snyder & Sickmund, 1999).
- Safe passages: Business owners offer students safe havens on their way to and from school in their businesses.
- Financial support: Business owners offer support in the form of equipment, supplies, facilities for events, and direct funding for school safety programs.

Content Application

This activity may be conducted for students or educators at a professional development session.

Educator application: Supply maps and sticky dots. Ask staff to place a dot were they grew up and attended school. Several dots may be provided, if the person has moved from school to school. Ask staff to reflect on a positive school experience from their childhoods. What were their fears associated with the school? How are those fears similar or dissimilar from those students are experiencing in the school today? What is their vision for a safe school, and how might one achieve it?

Student application: Ask students to think of a grade or age. Students are to reflect on one positive school experience. What were/are their fears associated with the school? What is their vision for a safe school, and how might one achieve it? Students may work in groups to draw their vision of a safe school and to brainstorm on how to achieve the goal.

DEFINING AN UNSAFE SCHOOL

A provision of No Child Left Behind (NCLB) requires states to define schools individually as "persistently dangerous." As a result of the unsafe school option legislation, states are using a variety of factors and approaches to identify unsafe, or "persistently dangerous," schools.

Persistently dangerous school indicators are provided below.

Persistently Dangerous School Indicators

Time period considered: Most states consider offenses or incidents occurring during a three-year period, while some consider a two-year period.

Threshold of offenses: Most states use a combination of a percentage of the student enrollment for some offenses and a specific number for other offenses, a specific number of offenses, or a percentage of the student population.

Offenses: Definitions of offenses/incidents vary to the extent of detail. A state using a narrowly defined list of offenses also may have a low threshold for the number of offenses, thus increasing the number of schools determined persistently unsafe. A state using a detailed offense list might have a high offense threshold resulting in a relatively low number of persistently dangerous schools.

In addition to the general indicators of persistently dangerous schools, states have created provisions such as the following:

Florida schools meeting certain criteria are required to conduct an anonymous schoolwide survey of students, parents, and personnel. If a majority (51 percent) of the survey respondents perceive the school as unsafe, the school is designated persistently dangerous.

In **Indiana**, a panel of local and state school safety experts determines if a school that has met the established criteria for the third consecutive year should be identified as persistently dangerous.

Schools identified as persistently dangerous in **Mississippi** and **North Dakota** have an opportunity, prior to final determination, to provide additional information to the state department of education or the state board of education.

South Dakota's policy considers all offenses occurring on school property, at school-sponsored events, or on buses—24 hours a day, 12 months a year—whether committed by or victimizing students, school personnel, or nonschool personnel.

In some cases, state policies involving the designation of persistently dangerous schools contain certain limits or exemptions. **Michigan** and **Tennessee,** for example, exclude alternative schools that have been created to serve suspended or expelled students.

Yet, is the NCLB provision useful in defining unsafe schools? A national survey found that only 54 schools nationwide were identified as dangerous (Robelen, 2003), and according to an August 19, 2003, article in *USA Today*, 44 states and the District of Columbia reported having no persistently dangerous schools (Toppo & Schouten, 2003). Do these statistics mean that few schools are unsafe or that the criteria for defining unsafe schools are too rigid, or might they reflect widespread underreporting by leaders fearful of the consequences of having an unsafe school classification? Indeed, further research is required in this area to determine if national, state, and local policies regarding unsafe schools should be altered.

Factors Associated With School Violence

In general, little agreement occurs in the literature as to the correlates of school violence. Research from criminal justice experts often points to changes in the juvenile justice system and accessibility to weapons as reasons for school violence, while mental health professionals point to the dissolution of the family, increases in family violence, and the growing trend toward risk-taking behaviors among youths as factors. According to Resnick et al. (1997), adolescents living in homes with easy access to guns are more likely to be involved in violent behaviors toward others. Zuckerman, Ausgustyn, Groves, and Parker (1995) note that children exposed to violence in the home may demonstrate long-term behavioral effects, including aggressive behaviors toward the self and others. The factors most often cited as possible correlates (across disciplines) include the following:

- Family factors, such as poor parenting skills as demonstrated by inadequate parental monitoring, inappropriate discipline techniques, or parental modeling of aggressive behavior
- Lack of individual social and coping skills and personality characteristics that would preclude propensity for violence
- Societal impact from the following:
  - School society: Includes peer relations and pressure, stress surrounding the need to succeed in school in the traditional capitalist/middle-socioeconomic-status climate, and poor school security measures
  - Larger U.S. society: Includes exposure to violence in media and entertainment, an increase in accessibility and use of guns, an increase in crime in general, and a decline in the moral character of the nation

In response to larger societal issues, educational institutions now serve a different socialization role for children than they did traditionally. Increasingly, educators perceive student deficits resulting from changes in the family and society and react by nurturing the social and physical development of students rather than merely the cognitive aspects of students. In striving to meet the needs of the "whole child" to better prepare a student academically, schools have had to increase their accountability to the three Rs plus! Now schools are seen as accountable for cognitive, social, and physical competence and are caught in the crossfire of controversy if students demonstrate a lack of skill or knowledge in any area of child development.

Most people agree that there isn't one single solution to school violence. Indeed, solutions might not be effective across students, schools, states, or the nation. Because changing the larger society or influencing family factors is perceived as more difficult and less immediate, a multilayer preventive education approach involving the school is currently the most realistic option for the problem of school violence (see Figure 1.1).

Clearly, the topic of school safety extends beyond the walls of educational institutions. Just as the underlying cause of school violence is not solely factors within a school, neither are the solutions for school safety the sole responsibility of school leaders. Instead, comprehensive school safety programs must include partnerships with the community. Representatives from juvenile justice programs, health and mental health professions, and religious organizations are only a few examples of individuals critical to the creation of safe schools.

Figure 1.1   Youth Violence as a Multilayer Problem

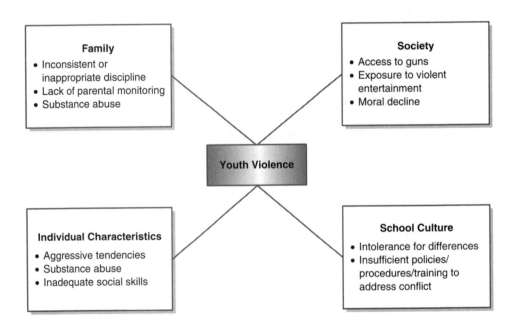

CHARACTERISTICS OF YOUTH OFFENDERS

In any school, three relatively distinct populations of students exist: (a) typically developing students, (b) those at risk for behavioral and academic problems, and (c) high-risk students who already manifest serious behavioral and academic difficulties (Sprague & Walker, 2000, 2005).

Although it is very difficult to predict whether students' behavior will lead to violence, school leaders should observe students' styles of conflict resolution, including avoidance of conflict situations. Researchers agree that most children who become violent toward themselves or others feel rejected and psychologically victimized. In most cases, children exhibit aggressive behavior early in life and, if not provided support, continue a progressive developmental pattern toward a severe aggression or violence. However, research also shows that when children have a positive, meaningful connection to an adult, whether at home, in school, or in the community, the potential for violence is reduced significantly.

School leaders should also consider the following warning signs, adapted from Dwyer, Osher, and Warger (1998):

- **Social withdrawal:** In some situations, gradual and eventually complete withdrawal from social contacts can be an important indicator of a troubled child.

- **Excessive feelings of isolation and being alone:** Research has shown that the majority of children who are isolated and appear to be friendless are not violent. However, in some cases, feelings of isolation and not having friends are associated with children who behave aggressively and violently.

- **Excessive feelings of rejection:** In the process of growing up, and in the course of adolescent development, many young people experience emotionally painful rejection. Some aggressive children seek out aggressive friends, who, in turn, reinforce their violent tendencies.

- **Being a victim of violence:** Children who have been victims of violence, including physical or sexual abuse in the community, at school, or at home, are sometimes at risk of becoming violent toward themselves or others.

- **Feelings of being picked on and/or persecuted:** The youth who feels constantly picked on, teased, bullied, singled out for ridicule, and humiliated at home or at school may initially withdraw socially. If not given adequate support in addressing these feelings, some children may vent them in inappropriate ways, possibly including aggression and violence.

- **Low school interest and poor academic performance:** Poor achievement can be the result of many factors. It is important to consider whether there is a drastic change in performance and/or performance becomes a chronic condition that limits the child's capacity to learn. In some cases, such as when the low achiever feels frustrated, unworthy, chastised, and denigrated, acting out and aggressive behaviors may occur.

• **Expression of violence in writings and drawings:** Children and youth often express their thoughts, feelings, desires, and intentions in their drawings and in stories, poetry, and other written expressive forms. Many children produce work about violent themes that for the most part is harmless when taken in context. However, an overrepresentation of violence in writings and drawings that is directed at specific individuals (family members, peers, other adults) consistently over time may signal emotional problems and the potential for violence.

• **Patterns of impulsive hitting and chronic hitting, intimidating, and bullying behaviors:** Children often engage in acts of shoving and mild aggression. However, some mildly aggressive behaviors, such as constant hitting and bullying of others, if left unattended, may later escalate into more serious behaviors.

• **History of violent, aggressive behavior and discipline problems:** Chronic behavior and disciplinary problems both in school and at home may suggest that underlying emotional needs are not being met. These unmet needs may be manifested in acting out and aggressive behaviors. These problems may set the stage for the child to violate norms and rules, defy authority, disengage from school, and engage in aggressive behaviors with other children and adults.

• **Intolerance for differences and prejudicial attitudes:** All children have likes and dislikes. However, an intense prejudice toward others based on racial, ethnicity, religion, language, gender, sexual orientation, ability, and/or physical appearance, when coupled with other factors, may lead to assaults against those who are perceived to be different. Membership in hate groups or the willingness to victimize individuals with disabilities or health problems also should be treated as early warning signs.

• **Drug use and alcohol use:** Apart from being unhealthy behaviors, drug use and alcohol use reduce self-control and expose children and youth to violence as perpetrators, as victims, or both.

• **Affiliation with gangs:** Gangs that support antisocial values and behaviors, including extortion, intimidation, and acts of violence toward other students, cause fear and stress among other students. Youth who are influenced by these groups, including those who emulate and copy their behavior as well as those who become affiliated with them, may adopt values and act in violent or aggressive ways in certain situations. Gang-related violence and turf battles are commonly tied to the use of drugs that often result in injury and/or death.

- **Inappropriate access to, possession of, and use of firearms:** Children and youth who inappropriately possess or have access to firearms can have increased risk for violence. Research shows that such youngsters also have a higher probability of becoming victims. Families can reduce inappropriate access and use by restricting, monitoring, and supervising children's access to firearms and other weapons. Children who have a history of aggression, impulsiveness, or other emotional problems should not have access to firearms and other weapons.

- **Serious threats of violence:** Idle threats are a common response to frustration. Alternatively, one of the most reliable indicators that a youth is likely to commit a crime is their talking about it.

- **A detailed and specific threat to use violence:** Recent indicators across the country clearly indicate that threats to commit violence against oneself or others should be taken very seriously. Steps must be taken to understand the nature of these threats and to prevent them from being carried out.

Leadership Strategies for Safe Schools is intended to support school leaders in developing proactive approaches to build safe schools. These approaches are intended for all youth in the school facility; however, it is important to note that proactive approaches may differentially affect students depending on a number of characteristics, including their propensity for violence. Understanding the characteristics of youth offenders and identifying potentially at-risk students are important steps toward building a safe school environment for all students.

2

Setting the Foundation

THE SCHOOL SAFETY TEAM

For a school leader, an important first step toward creating safer school communities is the development of a school safety team. In general, a school safety team is a group of individuals empowered by state or city government or school leadership to advise, guide, and respond to issues of school safety. School safety teams represent the community with a shared, comprehensive mission of producing a safer school and a better learning environment through a variety of means, including a school safety plan and crisis response plan. School safety teams, composed of members from diverse backgrounds but all involved in the school community, may be responsible for (a) developing a school safety plan, (b) assisting in the implementation of the plan, (c) facilitating the measurement of the effectiveness of the plan, and (d) reviewing and revising the plan according to changing school needs.

A school safety plan is a way for schools to address safety issues from a comprehensive, proactive, prevention-oriented approach that targets student factors, professional development of teachers, and involvement of community agencies (such as spiritual groups, youth-serving organizations, businesses, law enforcement, and so on). Drawing on school safety team members with various experiences and areas of expertise provides multiple perspectives on solutions to school violence and leads to a school safety plan that best addresses school needs and best facilitates the implementation of the plan in the school. If the correlates of school violence are widespread, then solutions must be as well.

Note that in many school systems, safe school teams handle both preventive approaches and reactive interventions to school safety issues;

however, this book focuses on preventive school safety initiatives. For instance, school safety teams might make recommendations for product-based approaches to school safety, such as metal detectors and video surveillance equipment. Although this chapter provides some guidance on these issues, the focus remains on school safety teams providing support and guidance for positive, process-based initiatives to enhance the school climate and student skills, knowledge, and attitudes. Teams should recommend implementation of specific educational programs in the schools, including conflict resolution education, peer mediation, in-school suspension programs; create policies and procedures regarding student and adult behavior associated with violence; seek appropriate funding for such programs; and develop community-school partnerships.

Composition of the School Safety Team

The school safety team should include representation from a number of different specialties and agencies with differing perceptions of school safety issues. The ideal team reflects the diversity of the community and the school and includes parents; perhaps a student or two; teacher(s); a school board member; a local government representative, such as the mayor or a city council member; a juvenile justice department representative, such as a judge or prosecuting attorney; city or county law enforcement officer(s); health and mental health specialists, such as a psychologist or school social worker; and community leaders from religious organizations and agencies that provide afterschool recreational activities, mentoring, tutoring, or cultural programs. It is most preferable for school safety teams to represent a school district rather than individual schools.

In selecting appropriate team members, the superintendent of schools traditionally leads the initiative; however, anyone may call for the creation of a school safety team, including the mayor or a justice department official. Regardless of who leads the process, the most critical element involves the makeup of the team. Team members don't need to be experts in the field of school safety or in school team leadership, but they should be committed to the concept of a safe school, appreciate that safe schools contribute to a positive learning environment, and recognize that their presence on the team is a commitment to social change.

The number of members of a school safety team varies according to the size of the community or school district; however, a good rule of thumb is no fewer than 10 members and no more than 25. Some suggestions for recruiting school safety team members appear in Figure 2.1.

Although safe school team members need not be experts in the field of school safety, it is critical that individuals who serve on the team receive some training in school safety issues from an outside consulting company. In particular, all team members should be involved in at least 10 to 20 hours of training on basic conflict resolution and collaborative problem solving. The more harmonious the group and the higher their level of

Figure 2.1   Recruiting School Safety Teams

Strategies for recruiting school safety team members include the following:

- Hosting an information meeting at the school for interested parents, teachers, and students.
- Speaking at city council and school board meetings about the school team.
- Announcing recruitment through local media, such as the newspaper and radio and TV stations.
- Recruiting interest through community policing efforts.
- Seeking recommendations (or recruits) from the closest university or other institution of higher learning.
- Posting information with local volunteer organizations that work within the school boundaries, such as the YMCA, YWCA, and Catholic Youth Organization (CYO).

knowledge and skill in the school safety area, the greater the likelihood the team will create appropriate school safety plans. One of the central tenets of the training and the school safety team is the view that conflict is positive and necessary for both internal and interpersonal growth and that violence, as one method of resolution, has clouded this fact. The training should also include the following:

- Conflict resolution education and its connection to academic competence and psychosocial benefits
- Violence as a multilayer problem, resolved through close collaboration with multiple groups
- Consensus-building and collaborative problem-solving techniques

Ideally, the school safety team should report only to school authorities, such as the school superintendent or, preferably, the school board. If, however, local government asks for the development of the school safety team, then the team might report to the local government or city council. Checks and balances occur within the group and not from outside the group. One of the most effective checks and balances is creating and following the timetable for implementing the school safety plan. The school safety team might select an informal leadership group that sets the meeting agendas, records and keeps meeting minutes, and serves as parliamentarians of meetings.

THE ROLE OF ASSESSMENT IN SCHOOL SAFETY

School safety plans depend on a thorough and accurate assessment of school safety needs. In fact, assessment provides the foundation for the school safety plan goals and objectives and for determining programming strategies. While school safety teams can certainly seek assistance with the needs assessment process by employing experienced consultants, administration and interpretation of the needs assessment provides valuable lessons for school safety teams in planning and modifying activities and programs.

Developing the School Safety Assessment Tool

The broadest purpose of the school needs assessment is to identify which of the four safety areas the school safety team must address. The secondary purpose of the needs assessment is to collect data useful for creating goals and objectives for the critical school safety areas.

Assessments must be complete, well developed, and tailored to the district or school. Too often, school leaders conduct an assessment using a tool devised by another school or researcher who doesn't ask the right questions of the right people. It is more economical and expedient and reaps results more specific to the school district if the school safety team creates the assessment tool. For this reason, it helps if the school safety team has a representative with some experience in assessment and evaluation, such as from the testing and measurement division of the school administration. If such an individual does not exist, the school safety team, rather than hire an outside consulting firm, should collaborate with a nearby university or local educational agency that has staff members experienced in a testing and measurement component.

In Michigan, for example, the state's mental health division conducts assessments in several communities for purposes of reducing school violence. A cadre of consultants knowledgeable in school safety issues from a mental health perspective, a criminal justice perspective, and a school administration perspective meets with community leaders, school representatives, students, parents, and business leaders. After three full days of discussion on school safety and the community, the consultants create an informal needs assessment tool based on the information provided by the interviews and offer preliminary recommendations for programming.

Ideally, school safety teams meet initially to discuss the needs assessment process and the content of the needs assessment tool. Most differences in assessments among schools are process differences—methods of data collection and number and type of personnel associated with the project. The assessment process includes deciding on the assessment timeline. Assessment should begin approximately two to four months before the school safety team convenes for development of the safe school plan. This period reflects the amount of time required to complete the needs assessment process using traditional methods of data collection, such as interview, questionnaire, archival information, and so on.

The team must also determine the personnel needed to create and complete the assessment for each stage of the process: preliminary data collection, complete data collection, and evaluation and application of assessment results.

Next, the team should understand the content of the assessment.

CONTENT OF THE SCHOOL
SAFETY ASSESSMENT TOOL

School safety team members must understand that they are on a fact-finding mission about areas of school safety and that the data they collect will provide guidance for recommendations for safer schools. Team members should remain objective: they should be careful to avoid personal agendas and to avoid anxiety that the results of the needs assessment might have long-term, negative repercussions. One school team, for example, chose not to collect juvenile crime statistics for the school campus and surrounding area. Although such information was vital to the needs assessment, and the data had not been collected for many years, team members were concerned about the possibility of negative statistics. They feared that the publication of negative statistics would produce ramifications such as a reduction of property values around the school. Nor should schools ignore an area of assessment merely based on perceptions held by the school team. For instance, the team should not overlook diversity issues even in relatively homogeneous communities with a lack of perceived student "differences." Unless an area has been addressed recently and with success, assessment should cover all areas of school safety.

Examples of Preliminary Data to Collect

School safety teams can begin the assessment process by gathering data already available through district, school, and other community sources. These data will inform the school safety team on areas of interest and potential areas of concern.

- General student and community demographic information: Available from the superintendent's office, these data are useful for assessing individual characteristics of the school population and the school community. Team members might collect data on students by age, gender, race, ethnicity, and number of years in the community. Information on socioeconomic status of families, number of single-parent households, and intergenerational households may also be helpful. These data assist team members in assessing personal and cultural characteristics of the school and community, the social environment of the school, and opportunities for school–community partnerships.
- Crime reports of individual schools or school districts: Crime reports obtained from local police departments might include type, location, and frequency of crimes occurring within the school, on school property, at school-related events, and in the school community. Data on the perpetrator and victims, including number of perpetrators, are also beneficial. The best source of information about nonfatal school-based violence derives from student self-report surveys. The Youth Risk Behavior Survey (YRBS) and the School Crime Supplement are rich sources of information. The purpose of collecting crime report information is to look for patterns (who, what, where, and how) of crime in the school community.

(Continued)

(Continued)

- Examples of student education programs currently in use in the classroom, school, or district: The school administration or teacher representative on the team can provide this information, which should include current initiatives, such as diversity youth groups and peer mediation programs, as well as past initiatives and, if possible, the results of the past initiatives. The information offers insight on individual level of exposure to knowledge and skills in the areas of conflict resolution education.
- Disciplinary and code of conduct regulations for the district, schools, and classrooms: Provided by the superintendent's office, individual school principals, and classroom teachers serving on the school safety team, these data are useful for individual and school community areas and assist team members in better understanding personal and cultural characteristics of the students and staff, the relationship (if any) to student education, and the political atmosphere of the school community.
- Safety and security policies of the school, city, county, and state: Often, the law enforcement representative can acquire this data in conjunction with the superintendent's office. These data are useful to assess intergroup, school community, and environment areas. Team members should identify procedures (if any) for responding to school and community crises and whether tracking systems for collecting data on safety issues related to the school and student population (number and type of crimes, location and time of offenses, offender and victim information, recidivism rates, etc.) are in place.
- Parent organization information on school safety: Obtained by the parent representative of the school safety team in conjunction with school representatives and the superintendent's office, these data are useful for assessing intergroup and school community issues. Particularly useful to collect for the needs assessment is the information provided to parents and new students on safe schools, discipline, and code of conduct.
- School architectural blueprints: Blueprints obtained from district plant engineering services or local government offices assist the team in its review of the school environment.
- Preliminary identification of current collaborative partnerships with law enforcement, criminal justice organizations, health and mental health agencies, and businesses: School safety team members provide these data, which, if possible, should include information on past collaborations and reasons for modifications in the partnerships.

ASSESSMENT AREAS

Stephens (1995) proposes six broad factors that contribute to a safe school and should be used in assessing levels of safe school needs. The following five factors, adapted from Stephens's model, are used for purposes of assessing school safety needs:

1. Cultural and personal characteristics of students and staff

2. Student and staff knowledge of, skills in, and attitudes toward peaceful conflict resolution

3. Social environment on campus

4. Local political environment surrounding the school

5. Physical environment of the school

Area 1: Cultural and Personal Characteristics

The needs assessment must contain address student and staff cultural characteristics. Cultural characteristics include one's values, assumptions, expectations, and ideologies. The team must identify and define these characteristics, because they tend to serve as foundations for behavior and perceptions regarding safe school environments. In general, cultural and ethnic differences occur with regards to issues of discipline, appropriateness of school behavior, and the responsibility of schools to "teach" moral conduct and behavior. Beliefs about the school's responsibility for teaching students to get along with others from different racial, ethnic, and cultural groups and for providing a safe learning environment impact school safety goals. Understanding expectations and assumptions of staff, students, and even parents assists in identifying programming strategies that meet the needs of the schools.

To assess the cultural diversity of the school, the school safety team should identify (1) all cultural, racial, and ethnic groups within the school and (2) the level of assimilation to the entire student population of each group. Specifically, school safety teams must clarify differences in cultural groups and, if the school has a large immigrant population, the nature of the immigration. For example, an assessment of student populations should identify recent immigrants, transitional immigrants (the families consider the community a stopover before moving to another community), and established immigrants.

Cultural characteristics play an important role in school safety. First, school policies on behavior requiring discipline in school might differ greatly from discipline practices in the home, and how to discipline can vary according to culture. Second, school violence may increase with cultural misunderstandings. Depending on the nature of the immigrant population, modifications in the school safety plan might have to occur more frequently so the school matches changes in student population (with transitory immigrant populations), or the school might need to develop new programs to match the student population (with new immigrant populations).

Case Study

The following example highlights why assessing the cultural characteristics of a school is important.

In a very diverse high school in metro Detroit, the school population consists of African-, Asian-, and Arab-American students along with a minority of White students. In this suburban school, the students are considered upper middle class. The school experienced a significant increase in physical conflict. Because of the highly diverse student population, school leaders had incorporated diversity education into the curriculum, but school violence continued and the program was ended.

Frustrated with the conflict, school leaders decided to perform a needs assessment. The assessment phase evaluated the social environment of the school, including identifying factions of students. Interviews with recent graduates revealed that conflict often occurred as a result of differences between the Arab-American Muslim student population and the Arab-American Catholic students. In fact, one hallway in one of the buildings marked the territories of the two groups, a school culture "fact" not known by school faculty. Students not associated with the hallway "owners" could not "pass" without repercussions, yet the hallway was the only interior corridor for passing from building to building. Students from the competing group could walk from building to building only if they used an alternate, exterior route. Predictably, conflict in the school increased in the winter months. Furthermore, these students divided themselves by the city of their family's origin and the number of immigrant generations (first-generation American, second-generation, and so on).

Assessments have to tease out the school culture because of its relevance to possible educational programming, as well as its relevance to possible links to community partnerships. As an example of the latter, the separated hallway in this case reflected the feelings of the parents of these students, which reduced the likelihood of constructive interpersonal relationships between parents of the two groups without school safety interventions. In the end, the school developed diversity training but with an emphasis on global issues, such as religious inclusiveness, in addition to race, culture, and so on for both students and parents. The hallway still exists, but students of both groups can pass freely, and conflict has decreased dramatically.

Assessing personal characteristics of students and staff also helps determine the relevance of school safety goals. For example, the assessment tool needs to inquire into previous experiences that might affect the school environment positively or negatively. Students and staff with highly negative personal experiences might perceive schools as sites of hopelessness and insecurity. Violent episodes occurring on the playground or on the way to and from school might reinforce these perceptions of unsafe conditions in the school. Safety issues at home might also affect a student's perception of safety at school. For example, if a student tells a teacher or counselor about abuse at home or implies that abuse is occurring, and school representatives choose not to address the issue without substantial evidence or they miss the cues, their lack of action might lead the student to inaccurate perceptions of safety in the school. In this type of situation, the school safety team should determine whether current policies and procedures contribute to unsafe conditions outside of the school. Might community partnerships help build safer environments for students? How does the school view intervention in cases of safety issues within the home? Individual students' assets, or the internal qualities and external conditions needed for young people to grow up to be healthy, caring adults, also should be included in the assessment (Sheldon & Epstein 2002). Answering these questions requires assessment of perceptions of students, staff, and parents.

Area 2: Knowledge, Skills, and Attitudes

The needs assessment must include data collection on student and staff knowledge of, skills in, and attitudes toward peaceful conflict resolution, diversity, and moral thought. These data guide the school safety team in its creation of goals and objectives for student learning, policy and procedures, and school–community partnerships. For instance, if students lack knowledge of and skills in conflict resolution, then the safe school team must develop a plan for implementing conflict resolution education to address this deficiency. Negative staff attitudes and lack of skills associated with working in diverse school populations might require professional development opportunities, as well as new school policies and procedures for diversity education.

To assess attitudes, a survey might ask respondents to rank (anonymously) the importance of variables such as specific elements of character and diversity education for students and professional development for teachers. As with students, staff members might possess negative attitudes toward certain racial or ethnic groups as a result of a number of factors, including ignorance about the group. Participation in professional development opportunities is one method to educate school staff about student diversity. School policies mandating diversity education or diversity committees increase the learning opportunities for both students and staff and, in turn, combat negative attitudes. For example, an increase in the number of ESL classes can lighten the load for many teachers in traditional classroom settings frustrated with large class sizes and increased numbers of ESL students and, at the same time, improve these teachers' attitudes toward diversity.

Staff perceptions of the school also influence school safety issues. Do school staff feel empowered to prevent acts of violence, or do school or district policies limit staff involvement? For example, school policies might prevent staff from breaking up a physical fight and mandate that school personnel leave the site to secure help from school security or local law enforcement. On the other hand, if staff members are required to intervene in student disputes, does this requirement produce uncertainty and anxiety for them? The physical and mental repercussions resulting from intervention in school violence not only affect staff perceptions of school safety, they affect behavior in the classroom of both teachers and students. When they know school policies limit adult intervention, students take greater liberties in the classroom. Conversely, authoritarian styles of teaching become more prevalent in schools that require intervention by staff members. The assessment might point to the need for educational programming related to personal defense strategies or anger and stress reduction to improve staff perceptions of an unsafe school.

Other questions the school safety team must discuss include how much responsibility school staff should take for stopping violent behavior in the hallways or in the parking lot. What is the responsibility of school staff toward teacher–student conflict? What do teachers consider and expect of a safe school? How should the school deal with conflict among staff members and between staff and students?

Often, the beliefs of members of the school community about the school's role in school safety issues depend on past personal experiences. An assessment question might ask whether school community members expect schools to be responsible for actions of others on the playground or during school-sponsored but off-site activities, such as athletic events. School safety team members need to know how the community views the role of the school in safety issues. Do parents and guardians believe that schools are only responsible for what happens within school walls, or do they believe the school has a responsibility toward the safety of students outside of the school, such as on the playground, at after-school events, and on the school bus. If parents believe that schools are only responsible for behavior within school walls, then team members should emphasize the assessment of issues within school walls.

Case Study

The following example highlights the importance of assessing knowledge of students, teachers, staff, and parent/guardians.

A small, nonpublic school in Vermont was experiencing heightened levels of absenteeism, decreased motivation, and increased classroom management issues among its sixth-grade students. As part of the safety team's needs assessment process, students, teachers, and parents/guardians were asked about their knowledge of bullying behaviors occurring in the school. Comparison of data collected through this process demonstrated (a) teachers and parents lack of knowledge surrounding the quantity, type, location, and intensity of bullying (relational and cyber) occurring in the school and (b) teachers, parents, and students lack of skills in intervening in bullying situations. The assessment process also highlighted students' indifference toward reporting bullying behaviors to teachers and parents/guardians as a result of the knowledge gap.

Area 3: Social Environment

School safety teams should measure the social environment of the school in relation to school safety needs. In most schools, there exists a social climate that can affect the success of school safety plans. For instance, in many schools, particularly high schools, students form cliques based on peer relations. These cliques tend to define school culture among students and, in many cases, define the school itself. Gangs are a destructive form of social cliques. School safety teams cannot ignore the issue of the social climate when proposing potential programs; therefore, team members must make themselves aware of the social networks in the school through the assessment process. As much as possible, information on the norms, mores, levels of trust, and codes of behavior among students and adults at the school should be collected (Cook, Murphy, & Hunt, 2000).

Usually, current students are the main source of information on the social environment of the school, but in some instances, team members should consult with recent school graduates to learn more about the strong "underground" networks. Questions to ask include What social cliques exist within the school? Are the cliques segregated by differences in socioeconomic status, physical ability, or academic status? Will school team recommendations affect some cliques more than others?

Case Study

In one case, school leadership learned about the school cliques but implemented a school safety tool that treated two social groups, the "druggies" and the "jocks," unequally, heightening conflict between them. The school implemented a tip hotline for school safety issues, and in the next year, druggies were consistently implicated falsely in school safety concerns through this hotline. Interviews with students revealed that members of the jocks clique were using the hotline to implicate the druggies just for fun. The druggies became more at odds with the more influential jocks and more distrustful of school leadership.

If school leaders had conducted an assessment of the school culture before recommending the hotline, they would have learned that the jocks were particularly vengeful against the druggies, and they could have addressed the issue either before establishing the hotline or certainly sometime that first year. A knowledge of school cliques and their degree of influence in the school is important to the school safety team planning phase.

In the area of educational programming, peer mediators must reflect the culture of the school (see Chapter 5). During the needs assessment phase, the school safety team should uncover as much as possible about the school social environment. By doing so, then if the team recommends a peer mediation program, the school already has information about what groups exist in the school, and representatives from every group can be selected as peer mediators.

Area 4: Political Environment

The needs assessment serves as a measure of the political environment surrounding the school. The political atmosphere reflects the external school community's perception of how to deal with school safety issues.

This differs from Area 2 (individual knowledge, skills, and attitudes). This assessment provides information on the level of support or amount of resistance to expect with regards to the school safety plan. For instance, do local government representatives support local schools and school safety issues? Do political leaders identify with the need to teach the "fourth R," *resolution* (constructive conflict resolution education), in the schools? Do local political platforms support character education and diversity?

The assessment tool should seek information on perceptions of the political atmosphere, as well as the true political atmosphere of a school community. Voter registration statistics may provide some information on the tendency of voters to lean in a political direction and, hence, to support certain issues. But assessing the perception of the political atmosphere requires input from parents, school faculty, and community leaders, including those responsible for the political atmosphere, such as local government and school board members. One way to evaluate perception is to identify any differences between responses of the political community and those persons not affiliated with the political community.

The results of the needs assessment may require that school safety teams plan goals for reshaping school policies and procedures to meet or combat the political atmosphere of the community. One reason for the strong recommendation that a local government member serve on the school safety team is to help gain support for the plan. Gauging and combating the political atmosphere is necessary only if the school team does not include this representation. Sometimes, the political agenda does not fit with the results of the assessment, particularly in the area of character education. As a member of the school safety team, the local government representative should be an unbiased party to the process. School teams may wish to gauge support for recommended policies that might contradict the political atmosphere.

Case Study

Consistent with proposed statewide legislation associated with student profiling, a New Mexico school district took steps toward providing professional development for teachers to spot potential problems and intervene with students identified as potential perpetrators of violence. Through the needs assessment process, the school safety team discovered strong local opposition to profiling students. Among the concerns raised by community members was the possibility of the proposed profiling policies violating students' rights, thus exposing the school district to potential lawsuits (based on discrimination).

Area 5: Physical Environment

The assessment must include a measurement of the physical environment. The physical environment of the school ranges from construction issues—such as the number of doors and windows, numbers of emergency-only exits, whether windows open or are sealed shut, campus size, and building size in relation to the student population—to issues of landscaping, indoor and outdoor lighting, and the distance from the school to emergency first responders. The assessment of the physical environment of the school directly affects the school safety improvement area of environment.

As a result of the needs assessment, school safety teams might learn of extensive loitering in high-traffic areas adjacent to the school or abandoned buildings representing serious safety issues for students on their way to and from school. School safety teams can address these issues quickly by creating goals and objectives related to building partnerships with local police departments or parent groups. Parents can place pressure on government officials to tear down abandoned buildings or on business owners to reduce loitering outside their businesses, as well as create safety networks to escort students past these buildings and businesses. In addition to the assessment of the physical environment outside of the school, the process might also uncover necessary improvements to internal building features. For instance, the needs assessment might draw attention to dark hallways or secluded classrooms, resulting in the school safety team creating goals associated with improving these environmental concerns through surveillance equipment.

Case Study

The fact is, often school leaders don't recognize that a dark hallway exists in the school or that it poses a school safety threat. One can compare this situation with conditions in one's own home. Say one of the stairs to the basement in a home has a loose board. The residents are so accustomed to the broken step that they have ceased to notice it. A visitor to the home, however, would consider this stair a serious hazard. The same is true of a school leader who walks the school every day but doesn't notice or recognize the hallway in a back wing as a possible safety concern.

Leadership of a newly constructed school in a large school district in California felt secure that the school had sufficiently addressed the physical safety of students. As a tag-on to their safety needs assessment, team members asked students for areas of the school building that they perceived as unsafe. Surprisingly, students consistently reported an unsafe area located in the front of the school. In this location, students reported violence, drug activity, and some gang activity. Upon inspection, the area in question could not be viewed by classroom windows or seen through outdoor surveillance cameras.

TECHNIQUES FOR MEASURING SCHOOL NEEDS

The technique selected to assess school needs is almost as important as the content of the assessment tool. Implementation of the assessment tool might be through methods such as focus groups, informal surveys, and interviews. Because these three methods provide school leaders and safe school teams with varying types and amounts of information, a combination of these methods is recommended to collect the most complete data on school safety needs. However, school safety teams should think about the amount of time available to collect data, recruitment of individuals to respond to the assessment tool, and type of data analyses and interpretation each method requires. A comparison of focus groups, informal surveys, and interviews appears in Figure 2.2.

As Figure 2.2 depicts, focus groups require the most time before program implementation compared with individual interviews and informal surveys. Focus groups require more time because this method requires recruiting participants, scheduling groups, administering the instrument, and analyzing the qualitative data. Since focus groups respond to questions in a group format, the composition of the group members is most important. Recruitment for surveys and interviews is not as sensitive because groups are not questioned together. Informal surveys, once developed, are administered and results interpreted in a relatively short time.

Usually, three people are required to administer the needs assessment through focus groups, whereas the interview and survey methods require fewer people to complete the process. Focus groups need two comoderators and one person responsible for taking extensive notes during the session. One or two people can conduct individual interviews, and one person can proctor informal surveys.

The number of participants involved in the needs assessment affects the number of persons necessary to administer the tool. Informal surveys may

Figure 2.2   A Comparison of Needs Assessment Data Collection Techniques

	Time Required Before Program Implementation	Minimum Number of Persons Required	Number of Participants	Resources for Data Analysis
Focus groups	At least eight weeks	Three	Groups of 10 participants	Requires qualitative data analysis skills
Individual interviews	At least four weeks	Two	One-on-one or two-on-one interviews	Requires qualitative data analysis skills
Informal surveys	At least two to four weeks	One	Large numbers of participants possible	Requires quantitative analysis skills

reach the greatest number of people, with individual interview techniques reaching the fewest. Depending on the size of the school and the anticipated breadth of the school safety improvement plan, participants in a needs assessment can range from 50 participants to 500. Five hundred participants equals 50 groups of 10 people each using focus groups, 500 individual interviews, and 500 informal surveys. The combination of time required and size of participant group may make informal surveys attractive. However, information gathered by means of informal surveys is limited to the questions asked of participants. Time spent creating the perfect survey covering all necessary information might have easily been spent moderating focus groups.

An example of a needs assessment survey aimed at school staff appears in Figure 2.3. This planning tool is particularly useful to help school teams identify the perceptions and culture of the staff regarding school safety issues. It also provides excellent guidelines for identifying the extent of current school partnerships and identifying relevant policies and procedures for student education and crisis management. School safety teams should pay careful attention to the items marked "To some extent" and "Not at all." The response "To some extent" indicates items school safety teams need to review. Newly created objectives or strategies might facilitate "Complete implementation" in the schools. On the other hand, the safe school team should address all items in the safe school plan marked "Not at all."

Figure 2.3   Planning Tool for School Staff: Ensuring Safety in Your School and District

The following tool is intended to guide the planning of school leaders and staff as they work to ensure safe schools for all students, school citizens, parents, and other educational stakeholders.

Strategic Plans for School Safety

	Completely implemented	To some extent	In development	Not at all
1. My school or district has a strategic plan in place that includes the warning signals of violence, in which ways they should be considered, what actions should be taken, and at what times.	❏	❏	❏	❏
2. My school or district has a team composed of school staff, students if age-appropriate, law enforcement personnel, community members, parents, and other educational stakeholders that meets regularly to discuss issues related to school safety and violence prevention/reduction.	❏	❏	❏	❏

(Continued)

Figure 2.3 (Continued)

	Completely implemented	To some extent	In development	Not at all
3. Professional development in my school or district focuses on issues related to school safety and violence prevention/reduction and is in-depth and sustained rather than sporadic.	❏	❏	❏	❏
4. Each staff member in my school or district has a contingency plan in place should violence or disruption erupt in one of our classrooms or on school grounds.	❏	❏	❏	❏
5. My school or district has procedures in place to ensure that local law enforcement personnel are kept apprised of school and/or district safety plans, as well as reports of disruptive or violent incidents.	❏	❏	❏	❏

Violence Prevention/Reduction

	Completely implemented	To some extent	In development	Not at all
1. My school or district has a violence prevention/reduction curriculum in place that is integrated throughout content areas at all grade levels.	❏	❏	❏	❏
2. My school or district has a climate that recognizes student contributions toward making the school a safe and productive learning place.	❏	❏	❏	❏
3. My school or district emphasizes training and professional development in violence prevention/reduction for all school staff.	❏	❏	❏	❏
	Always	To some extent	In development	Not at all
4. Staff at my school or in my district know the warning signs of potential violence and consult calmly but immediately with other staff—or contact local authorities—if these warning signs are present.	❏	❏	❏	❏
5. At the individual level, professional development in my school or district has sensitized me to my own anger and ways of dealing with conflict.	❏	❏	❏	❏

Community Outreach and Collaboration

	Always	To some extent	In development	Not at all
1. My school or district works actively to engage community organizations, parents, and law enforcement personnel in the strategic planning process to ensure school safety in my community.	❏	❏	❏	❏

		To	In	Not
2. My school or district has a team composed of community members, parents, law enforcement personnel, and other educational stakeholders that meets regularly to discuss ongoing issues related to school safety and violence prevention/reduction.	*Always* ❑	*some extent* ❑	*development* ❑	*at all* ❑
3. The school board in my community regularly discusses violence prevention and reduction in a proactive, rather than reactive, manner.	*Always* ❑	*some extent* ❑	*development* ❑	*at all* ❑
4. As a teacher or administrator, I find ways to infuse the awareness of violence and the ways in which it can escalate into my daily lesson plans in ways that do not frighten students but are age-appropriate and develop their awareness of our violent society.	*Always* ❑	*some extent* ❑	*development* ❑	*at all* ❑
5. The material that I teach in my classroom de-emphasizes violence as a solution to everyday problems and seeks positive solutions to the resolution of conflict.	*Always* ❑	*some extent* ❑	*development* ❑	*at all* ❑

Community Violence Prevention/Reduction

		To	In	Not
1. The staff in my school or district works to make school safety a positive issue rather than something negative and frightening to students, staff, and other educational stakeholders.	*Always* ❑	*some extent* ❑	*development* ❑	*at all* ❑
2. My school or district recognizes that we need the cooperation of law enforcement personnel, community agencies and organizations, parents, and other educational stakeholders— and has a proactive plan to secure their collaboration.	*Always* ❑	*some extent* ❑	*development* ❑	*at all* ❑
3. If I have concerns about school safety, my school or district has ensured that I know at least two individuals outside my school environment whom I can call for help and advice.	*Always* ❑	*some extent* ❑	*development* ❑	*at all* ❑
4. Suggestions from community groups, law enforcement personnel, and other educational stakeholders regarding school safety are taken seriously and encouraged in my school or district.	*Always* ❑	*some extent* ❑	*development* ❑	*at all* ❑

(Continued)

Figure 2.3 (Continued)

	Always	To some extent	In development	Not at all
5. The staff in my school or district works to make the school a calm place where learning can take place undisturbed by bullying, harassment, or other indicators of potential violence.	❑	❑	❑	❑

SOURCE: Reprinted with permission from Dr. Anne Turnbaugh Lockwood (1999).

A second example of a needs assessment tool for school staff appears in Figure 2.4. The assessment tool in Figure 2.4 differs because it demonstrates a measurement method for follow-up to a preliminary needs investigation. For example, in conducting a cursory needs assessment of the four school safety improvement areas, team members identify that students' knowledge, skills, and attitudes regarding peaceful conflict resolution are somewhat deficient. However, they need more information about what programs to recommend. Figure 2.4 represents a follow-up measure to support the development of goals pertaining to student education on conflict resolution.

Figure 2.4   Needs Assessment

Safety Improvement Areas: Student Education

Topic: Conflict Resolution Education

Program goals and objectives:

- In what ways would a violence prevention program help prevent and resolve conflict?
- What kind of violence prevention program should the school develop and implement?
- Is behavioral, cognitive, and/or attitudinal change among students and staff desired?*

Obstacles:

- What constraints must the program overcome to be successful?

Staffing:

- Who will coordinate and participate in the program?
- Is the staff knowledgeable about all relevant issues of violence prevention, or is professional development needed?
- Will professional development involve the whole school or only the school staff members involved with the recommended program?
- Is the staff willing to participate?

Funding:

- How much money will it take to implement, maintain, and evaluate the program?
- Where will the school seek funding?

Resources:

- To what extent will parents play a role in the violence prevention program?
- Can the school develop and implement the program on its own, or will it need to retain a consultant?
- Can the school evaluate the program on its own, or does it need to retain a consultant?
- What additional community resources are necessary to ensure program success?

* This assessment is primarily for school faculty and other staff. When surveying parents and older students, possible substitutions for this question might be the following: What benefits do you think would occur following the implementation of a violence prevention program? or What do you think students should learn from violence prevention programs?

Costs associated with each of the three techniques vary. Focus group methods require hiring experienced consultants to facilitate the groups. In addition, volunteers participating in the focus groups occasionally receive small tokens of appreciation. Similarly, interviewers require payment, and interview subjects might also receive tokens. Surveys are often the most economical technique for assessing school needs. School leaders should expect to provide small tokens to survey participants and to cover costs associated with typing and duplicating the surveys.

THE ARGUMENT FOR FOCUS GROUPS

Focus groups are group interviews that are structured and purposeful, usually moderated by a professional skilled in interviewing techniques. Focus groups use face-to-face interactions for gathering data, while surveys (both informal and formal) traditionally do not require this. Surveys ask respondents the same questions in the same order with set follow-up questions. Focus groups allow a great deal of flexibility in questions: respondents might provide answers to some questions but not to all or to some questions with considerable follow-up questions. In general, the use of focus groups is a more open-ended approach than surveys, and it is based on the strength of qualitative data analysis, while surveys depend on quantitative methods of analyses.

The single most important reason for using focus groups is to address school safety issues from a variety of perspectives. People view school safety differently, and focus groups allow data collection from multiple perspectives; namely, in focus groups, people support others' perspectives and accrue support for their beliefs. This evolution and interactiveness does not occur with the other methods. For instance, although school safety is the common goal for focus group representatives, some participants may state a need for conflict resolution education, while others prefer improving school environment factors to improve school safety. The fact that the group maintains a common goal of school safety, although diverging on ways to achieve this goal, provides a level of comfort within the group, encouraging truthfulness in responses. A well-trained moderator provides an encouraging environment in which participants feel free to speak. The other survey methods are not interactive or engaging. The interview technique poses questions but does not challenge responses.

Focus groups are also useful to bridge gaps among groups of people. For instance, bringing parents and teachers together in a focus group format exposes both groups to the other's needs. The group provides immediate feedback on proposed strategies advocated by parents and opposed by teachers or vice versa. The process of resolving differences concerning the safety school goals is extremely important information for school safety teams when developing strategies acceptable to multiple parties.

Tips on administering school safety focus groups appear in Figure 2.5, and sample focus group questions from the American Institute for Research (Quinn, Osher, Hoffman, & Hanley, 1998) appear in Figure 2.6.

Figure 2.5   Tips for Focus Group Success

- **Pay attention to the diversity of group members in school safety assessment.** Placing school staff and school administration together may not reap as much information as placing school staff with parents. Similarly, a group made up solely of students and parents is not the best mix. Place mental health professionals with school staff, parents with criminal justice experts, and school administrators with policy or government personnel in the same focus groups. Also, success of focus groups depends on the comfort level of individuals within the group. Keep in mind that hierarchical difference, whether perceived or real, affects information reaped from the sessions.

- **Don't represent the outcomes of the focus groups as objectives that will be implemented.** Too often, people are asked their opinions, then don't see action on these issues. Be clear with focus group representatives that the focus groups' purpose is to gather information, not interpret the information. The school safety team will use focus group results to create goals and objectives of the safety school plan, but some of the topics discussed might not be included at all. Inform participants that their responses might influence goals and objectives, but they will not determine strategies for implementation.

SCHOOL SAFETY PLAN

Once the school safety team has been convened and a needs assessment completed, a school safety plan must be created. The school safety plan generally covers four areas: (1) environmental safety, (2) student education, (3) school policies and procedures, and (4) school–community partnerships. Schools that have outdated or nonexistent school safety plans should address all four of the school safety issues. In other cases, however, school safety teams might determine that they need not address all four areas simultaneously but can address them in a staggered fashion instead. For instance, the team might develop plans for student education one semester and environmental concerns the following semester.

Area 1: Environmental Safety

School safety teams may wish to create plans for environmental safety that address a variety of factors, including access control, surveillance, and

Figure 2.6   Focus Group Questions

Students

1. What is your name, and what grade are you in?
2. What do you like most about your school?
3. What do you like least about your school?
4. Do you feel safe at school?
5. What are the most important things that the adults at your school do to make you safe?
6. What are the rules for how to behave at school?
7. Did kids help come up with these rules?
8. Do you think it's important for kids to be involved in helping set the rules?
9. What do your teachers do to help you remember and follow the rules?
9a. What other adults help you remember and follow the rules, and what do they do?
10. If you or a friend had a serious problem, to whom at your school would you go for help?
11. What advice can you give us to help students behave better?
12. What advice can you give us to help make schools safer?

Family Members

1. Please take one minute to introduce yourself (6 minutes).
2. What do you see as the three major discipline and school safety-related problems at your child's school? (6 minutes)
3. What does your child's school do to support appropriate behavior and promote safe schools for your child and other children? (15 minutes)
4. How are parents involved in your child's school's attempt to create a safe and orderly environment that promotes learning and development? (15 minutes)
5. What can the rest of the nation learn from your child's school about making schools safe and drug-free environments that promote learning and development? (15 minutes)

Special Educators/Related Service Personnel

1. Please introduce yourself, stating your grade level or subject area. Briefly state the three most common discipline problems at your school. (5 minutes)
2. Among students with disabilities, what are the key things that are done at your school to support positive student behavior, and who are the key players in implementing these? (16 minutes)
3. What impact have these measures had? (16 minutes)
4. What would it be like at your school without these services and supports? (6 minutes)
5. What can special educators or related service providers across the nation learn from your school about making schools safe and drug-free for all students? (16 minutes)

(Continued)

Figure 2.6 (Continued)

Regular Educators

1. Please introduce yourself, stating your grade level or subject area. Briefly state the three most common discipline problems at your school. (5 minutes)

2. What are the key things that are done at your school to support positive student behavior, and who are the key players in implementing these? (16 minutes)

3. What impact have these measures had? (16 minutes)

4. What would it be like in your school without these services and supports? (6 minutes)

5. What can teachers across the nation learn from your school about making schools safe and drug-free for all students? (16 minutes)

Administrators/School Board Members

1. Please introduce yourself and tell us what you think are the three major discipline and school safety-related problems in your school district. (10 minutes)

2. What are the key things that are done in your district to support positive student behavior, and who are the key players in implementing these? (15 minutes)

3. What would it be like in your school without these services and supports? (5 minutes)

4. What do you see as the major barriers to collaboration, and what can federal, state, and local officials do to eliminate them? (15 minutes)

5. What can administrators and school board members across the nation learn from your district about making schools safe and drug-free for all students? (15 minutes)

Change Agents/Agency Representatives

1. Please introduce yourself and tell us what you see as your role in helping create safe and drug-free schools that support learning and development. (15 minutes)

2. What are the key things that you do to support schools' efforts to create safe and drug-free schools that support learning and development? (15 minutes)

3. What do you see as the major barriers to collaboration, and what can federal, state, and local officials do to eliminate them? (15 minutes)

4. What are the lessons that people like you and other communities can learn from your experiences working in/with schools? (15 minutes)

SOURCE: Quinn, M. M., Osher, D., Hoffman, C. C., & Hanley, T. V. (1998). *Safe, drug-free, and effective schools for ALL students: What works!* Washington, DC: Center for Effective Collaboration and Practice, American Institutes for Research.

general security measures. Needs assessment data collected by school safety team members will inform the development of environmental safety planning.

Access control consists of measures to control entrance to or exit from the school premises by locking certain access points from the inside to prevent outside access or creating traffic flow patterns so students only enter and exit certain doors. The team should evaluate the number of campus entrances and exits and suggest ways to reduce the number of access points to campus or control student traffic through existing entrances. Closing high school campuses during school hours simplifies surveillance demands and helps prevent entry by unauthorized persons. Teams may consider identification badges for visitors, staff, and students that are to be worn at all times. Badges may be coded for access to the school facility.

Under surveillance measures, the team might call for installation of surveillance equipment and monitors in hallways, cafeterias, and outside parking areas to have clear views of these areas. Strategically placed cameras can be a deterrent by themselves and may assist in identifying intruders. General security measures include guards, metal detectors, and landscaping control. Schools increasingly use either sworn officers or community safety personnel to supervise students, provide training, and intervene in conflicts or illegal activity.

Communication strategies should be included in the safe school plan. All adults in the school should have the ability to achieve two-way communication with the front office at all times, without leaving the classroom or otherwise entering a dangerous situation. Building emergency procedures should be reviewed with staff each fall, contained in the staff handbook, and practiced by all staff and students, much like the traditional fire drill. The school should make available a confidential reporting system for anyone during school or nonschool hours. Options include anonymous "tip lines" or Web-based applications, such as Report It (www.report-it.com).

Safety teams can also recommend a review of school landscaping and school architecture that might influence school safety. Perhaps the most neglected source of vulnerability is the architectural design of the school building and surrounding grounds (Schneider, Walker, & Sprague, 2000). School safety and security were not dominant concerns when most current school facilities were designed. However, the knowledge base required for designing safer schools has existed for some time. This knowledge has been organized and formulated into a set of principles known as Crime Prevention Through Environmental Design (CPTED). CPTED has been applied with considerable effectiveness in making school sites safer and more secure in recent years (Schneider, Walker, & Sprague).

Structural issues include darkened, isolated hallways, classrooms, staircases, and restrooms. Landscaping must be maintained; for example, bushes should not interfere with school access points or with visibility of students on the playground or in the parking lot. They should be cut far below the windows of the school or be planted away from school walls.

Area 2: Student Education

School safety teams develop safety plans that address educational programming for students. As part of its role to determine the goals and objectives for educating students on constructive methods of conflict resolution, the team identifies what type of conflict resolution education is necessary. The term *conflict resolution education* describes methods for teaching students to resolve interpersonal conflicts constructively. The team might select a social skills program that the school adds to the curriculum, social skills training that teachers infuse into the current curriculum, or even a specific conflict resolution program, such as peer mediation. In schools with conflict resolution educational programming already in place, the team reviews and recommends modifications based on current student outcomes and program effectiveness: the team looks for changes in student knowledge, skills, and attitudes related to antiviolence concepts. The team also measures school incidents of violence and other behavioral change indices.

As a result of the needs assessment, safety teams may recommend that the school safety plan include several types of educational initiatives. For instance, the team might identify heightened tension in a diverse student population and a growing trend of segregated peer groups, as reported by team members (school faculty, administration, parents, and students), and recommend violence prevention education and diversity education as essential components for school safety.

The team must address the student education needs but must also consider the supporting research evidence and the cultural, and developmental appropriateness of the program. In addition, the school safety team should identify the type and amount of professional development required for school staff and support personnel to teach conflict resolution education and help create a safer learning environment for more information on professional development opportunities).

Area 3: School Policies and Procedures

School policy and procedure revision and development form a possible third component of school safety plans. School safety teams should review current school policies and procedures regarding student and staff behavior and discipline and develop appropriate policies and procedures. Working within the context of state and local laws and school board governing policies and using other schools' policies as models, the team might adopt new and needs-driven policies for specific school safety issues. An example of a policy agreement created by the Michigan Department of Education, the state Superintendent of Public Instruction, the Michigan State Police, and the Michigan Attorney General appears in Appendix B to assist school safety teams in outlining school safety information sharing among members of the school, law enforcement, and juvenile justice representatives. Members of the school safety team should also create and review policies supporting crisis management plans. Adaptations to school policies and procedures will be greatly informed by the needs assessment data collected by the members of the school safety team. Conduct policies, behavioral definitions, and adaptations of behavioral discipline policies, such as the zero-tolerance policy for student violence, are necessary in any school safety plan.

Area 4: School–Community Partnerships

The school safety team should consider including in the school safety plan objectives for building program collaboration with local law enforcement, health and mental health agencies, and the business community. In creating these partnerships, teams should consider mechanisms for garnering support for initial program goals through public awareness campaigns and techniques for maintaining productive collaborations. Mechanisms for garnering support include having team members introduce basic program goals to groups involved with schools and community-based agencies and organizations. Techniques for maintaining productive collaborations include planning for expansion of the current partnerships, enhancing leadership training for the collaborative partners, celebrating accomplishments, and adding innovations.

School safety teams should also consider developing plans for legislative support of school safety initiatives. Again, teams should devise a plan that addresses who will be involved with creating the school partnerships with community and government agencies, the goals and expectations of the collaboration, and the strategies that will ensure the success of the relationships.

DEVELOPING SCHOOL SAFETY PLAN STRATEGIES

Once the school safety team has decided to focus on environmental issues, student education programs, school policies and procedures, or school-community partnerships, the next step is to plan strategies to improve school safety areas. Although the how of school safety plan development occasionally differs by school team, the general components of developing strategies remain similar. The strategies for each of the selected safety areas should have the following components:

- Vision
- Statement of need
- Goals and objectives
- Timeline for implementation and evaluation
- Procedures for plan review
- Resources required to implement school safety programs

Vision

The first responsibility of a school safety team is to define its vision of a safe school, strategies for achieving the safe school, and possible obstacles in the development of the safe school. This exercise serves as the foundation for continuing with the remaining components. Figure 2.7 provides some interesting insight into how representatives from different agencies define their visions of a safe school.

Figure 2.7   Perceptions of Safe Schools

Safe school team members may have different perceptions of a safe school, and understanding these differences in perception is critical to the teams working together collaboratively. One way to discern these different perceptions is for team members to draw their vision of the safe school on a blank sheet of newsprint. Team members collaborate on how the safe school might appear without using words. The results of one such activity yielded some fairly typical results.

In this case, team members representing school leaders did not differ greatly in their ideas of the image of a safe school compared with members of a team representing law enforcement, yet their depiction of methods for achieving safe schools did differ. School leaders were more inclined to represent safe schools as possessing strong parent involvement, clean learning environments, and strong leadership. Law enforcement representatives' visions included police presence on campus for educational, not security, purposes and strong involvement of students in extracurricular activities. Both groups drew students involved with peaceful conflict resolution. Interestingly, the safe school image containing metal detectors and surveillance equipment was not reflected in either group's pictures.

As a follow-up to the activity, school safety teams should think of the strategies necessary to create their "ideal" images of the safe school and what obstacles they may face before achieving these goals.

The school safety team should begin developing strategies for plan implementation through a vision statement. This statement should clearly incorporate all members' perceptions of the safe school and how the team can achieve the vision.

Statement of Need

School safety teams should develop a statement of need for each of the school safety areas identified as necessary areas of concentration by the assessment-of-needs tool. The needs assessment helps school safety teams define strategies for implementing programming initiatives aimed at the school safety areas.

Goals and Objectives

When the school safety team has completed the vision statement and identified the needs of the school and community, the team proceeds to the third component—identifying measurable goals and objectives for the school. The team should create goals and objectives for each of the school safety areas identified in the needs assessment as essential to the school safety plan.

Goals, broadly defined, are the purposes proposed for school safety. Goals serve as generalized statements of how students' behaviors and ways of thinking will change following the implementation of the school safety plan. Objectives are the measurable steps required to accomplish the goal: they answer who, what, where, and how.

School safety teams should invest a great deal of time in developing goals and objectives because they serve as yardsticks of programming success or failure. Goals and objectives need not specify every action of school safety programming; instead, they should outline manageable steps to evaluate and revise if needs of the school change. School leaders creating their first school safety plan should limit goals to five to ten short-term goals and five to seven long-term goals for each school safety area.

A sample goal for the student education school safety area appears in Figure 2.8. As the figure depicts, goals focus on only one aspect of school safety issues and use specific language. The measurable objectives follow the goal statement. They, too, are stated specifically, making goal achievement easy to measure. A poorly defined school safety goal and objective appears in Figure 2.9.

As the figures depict, school safety teams should set achievable goals. For instance, one school safety team created the goal of eliminating conflict in the schools. Completely eliminating conflict in the schools is an unrealistic, unobtainable goal. In turn, its nature affects the probability of success of the measurable steps designed to achieve the goal. How might any school safety team plan to eliminate conflict in the school? No strategies will ever be available to meet this school safety team goal. Not only are

Figure 2.8   Sample Measurable Goals Outline—School District #4

School safety area: Student Education

Short-term (one-year) goal: Increase by 25 percent (two schools) the number of schools using peer mediation training as violence prevention programming.

Measurable objectives (*Note:* Language of objectives is active but not authoritarian.):

1. Identify at least three schools open to peer mediation training program implementation.
2. Recruit students and staff to undergo training in conflict resolution and peer mediation techniques.
3. Provide orientation to students and staff in peer mediation principles.
4. Publicize the peer mediation program to parents and students through meetings and newsletters. (Students feel more comfortable using the mediation services if the program is well publicized, and parents need to know about the program to eliminate any misunderstandings about it.)
5. Implement program by January 1 of new year.

Figure 2.9   Sample Inappropriate Measurable Goals Outline—School District #4

School safety area: Student Education

Short-term (one-year) goal: Reduce conflicts in the school.

Measurable objectives: Buy conflict resolution curriculum for all fourth- and fifth-grade teachers.

unrealistic goals a waste of time, but, more importantly, unsuccessful objectives can also interfere with safety team commitment and motivation to continue with safe school programming. Instead, safe schools teams should produce realistic goals—for example, reducing violent interpersonal conflict by 30 percent over two years—and create appropriate measures to achieve these goals.

Having carefully and clearly defined goals and objectives in the school safety plan also helps when seeking supportive funding for the project, as funding agencies often require clear, concise methods for measuring programming success. Finally, the team must agree on primary goals and objectives.

The goals and objectives created by the school safety team should name a variety of programs and strategies to achieve the recommended goals and objectives. Plans should always include numerous options for programming, as one technique will not meet the needs of all students. School safety teams should provide a mixture of objectives that meet the needs of the general school population and the at-risk population—youths prone to aggressive behavior to self or others, violence, and delinquency. In identifying the program or strategy to accompany each objective, teams should consider the following:

- Does the planned program or strategy support the overall goals and objectives of the school safety plan?
- Is the proposed program or strategy developmentally appropriate? In other words, does the program or strategy fit the cognitive, social, and physical abilities of the intended age group?
- Is the proposed program or strategy appropriate for the school population and its diverse learning styles and abilities?
- Has the proposed program or strategy been evaluated empirically, and what successes have been demonstrated in similar school safety programs and similar student populations? (Subsequent chapters recommend programs and highlight empiric findings if available. Appendix C provides additional resources.)
- Is the proposed program or strategy culturally sensitive?
- Does the planned program or strategy appear to provide consistent results over time?

Timeline for Implementation of the School Safety Plan

Members of the team must also consider the timeline for implementation of the school safety plan. Will implementation of the school safety plan take place at the beginning of the school year, or will it begin sometime after the beginning of the school year? How long will it take to share the outcomes of the school safety plan with school faculty and notify parents and students of the proposed goals and objectives? The school safety team members must also decide if certain programs and strategies should be implemented earlier while others should be implemented later. For instance, school safety team members might recommend an immediate implementation of the crisis response plan and a later implementation of a diversity council for students. In addition to a timeline for goals and objectives, the team must also consider a timeline for evaluating and reviewing the school safety plan.

Procedures for Plan Review

School safety team members should conduct a careful review of school safety programming. At least 75 percent of team members should return to assist in the review and possible revision of the safety plan. (While, ideally, the school team will remain intact over time, school safety teams, like any other loosely organized group, will have attrition.) School safety plans must be reviewed at a minimum of once per year; however, teams must also revisit safety plans when evaluation information suggests that proposed programs or strategies are not meeting the goals and objectives of the program.

An evaluation may conclude that the school safety team needs to address all four school safety areas in the next year or that the team needs address only two safety areas. Perhaps the evaluation will result in the school safety team's addressing school budget issues. Safety teams might advise that the school board review budget issues pertaining to safety programs suggested in the plan. The school safety team usually does not write the grants (school district representatives do it) but provides suggestions for seeking funding. For more on evaluation, see the section Evaluating Safety Plan Effectiveness.

Resources Required to
Implement School Safety Programs

Finally, the school safety team should consider resources needed to implement the school safety program. A clear budget for school safety program implementation should be created. The budget should include personnel, curriculum purchases, evaluation costs, and funds to disseminate program outcomes. Team members may identify current resources that can be redirected to meet the needs of the school safety plan or research opportunities for implementing the school safety plan.

IMPLEMENTING THE
SCHOOL SAFETY PLAN

Once the school safety team has developed the safety plan, team members should facilitate the plan's implementation in the schools. Although team members most likely are not involved directly in implementing strategies associated with school policies or conflict resolution education, they play a critical role in building faculty, student, parent, and community consensus for school safety program development. Publicity supporting the program at school PTA meetings, at inservice workshops, and through public relations and media efforts assists in the ease of program implementation. The purpose of the publicity campaign is to inform the public about the team and its objectives and get public support. Typically, the school safety team hands the plan off to the superintendent's office, which promotes the plan. But team members are critical for word-of-mouth publicity. The team should share the results of the needs assessment with school faculty and describe the school safety plan and its goals, objectives, and vision before implementation.

Including school faculty in decisions concerning implementation is also crucial to program success, particularly if the plan proposes conflict resolution education implementation or revision. In many schools, school faculty members and administration commit to supporting the initiatives by signing safe school commitments, informal agreements that demonstrate teachers' commitment to investing considerable time in and supporting school safety initiatives. Depending on faculty union contracts, however, some schools do not require written school commitments, preferring informal commitments by teachers, who agree that school safety issues are critical to constructive learning environments and agree to promote safe schools in their classrooms.

EVALUATING SAFETY PLAN EFFECTIVENESS

Traditionally, team members review school safety plans annually, and programming evaluation occurs concurrently with program implementation. The school district's internal evaluation team often performs this evaluation in conjunction with the school safety team. Sometimes, the district hires outside consultants to perform the evaluation, or school safety team members assist a university partnership or internal school district evaluation team with the collection of data to measure the effectiveness of the school safety plan.

School safety teams should plan to collect data at least three times during the first programming year. Evaluation components should include an opportunity to collect baseline data related to skills, knowledge, and attitudes regarding conflict, conflict behavior, and violence two months before proposed program or strategy implementation. Then data collection should take place two months after initial program or strategy implementation and again six months after the initial program or strategy implementation. Member representatives from health and mental health agencies can collect information on numbers of criminal/violence cases referred to them. Local police officials can assist in collecting data on crime statistics in and around schools and their effect on neighborhood structure. Chapter 7 provides complete program evaluation information.

The evaluation results may suggest the use of different approaches, the need for additional training of staff, or the need for outside assistance from professional evaluators or a partnership with a university or other organization. Review and revision of school safety plans must be ongoing and responsive to the ever-changing environment. Important plan evaluation and review questions include the following:

- How well are the objectives moving the school toward the team's goals?
- What other strategies might the school use to meet the goals?
- Should the goals change to reflect new school safety issues?
- What obstacles occurred in implementing these goals, and what methods can the school use to overcome these obstacles?

3

Positioning Character Development in School Curricula

EFFECTS OF CHARACTER ON SAFE SCHOOLS

Safe schools are built, in part, by personal decisions students make every day in classrooms, in hallways, and on the playground. They choose ways to resolve intrapersonal conflicts by deciding how to act, react, and think. For instance, a student is offered a stolen copy of an upcoming math test. The student really has to do well on the test to pass the class. Does the student accept the stolen test and cheat, or does the student reject the offer and take the test without the assistance of the stolen material? Or perhaps a student jumps in front of another student in the cafeteria line and takes the last dessert available. What does the student do about the "dessert snatcher"? Does the student retaliate and attack the other student physically or verbally? Ignore the actions and retreat? Talk it out with the other student? How do students decide to resolve these intrapersonal conflicts? How do these students choose to do the "right" thing?

The opportunity to cheat on an exam and to retaliate for unkind actions are two examples of intrapersonal, or internal, conflict that students face each day. How they resolve these intrapersonal conflicts can affect their interpersonal relationships and conflicts and have significant effects on the development and establishment of safe schools. Students must be prepared to resolve intrapersonal conflicts and understand that their decisions have consequences interpersonally. What would schools look like if all students resolved interpersonal conflicts with peaceful conflict resolution methods? Students' knowledge and demonstration of the "right" actions or thoughts is strongly based on the concept of character.

> ***Character education.*** Broadly, character education encompasses all aspects of the influence that families, schools, and other social institutions have on the positive character development of children and adults.

CHARACTER EDUCATION

Character education programs have become increasingly connected to safe school planning in schools across America. Chronically violent youth have been framed as students with moral defects. As acts of violence have increased among youth, school leaders have struggled diligently with strategies to prevent tragic events in their schools. One proposed solution to reduce the potential for school violence is to provide character education programs to students in elementary and secondary grades. In fact, Congress has provided significant funding for schools to implement character education programs both during and after school hours.

Character education programs emphasize the development of character, which Likona (1991) defines as three interrelated parts: moral knowing, moral feeling, and moral behavior. Broadly defined, *character* is an individual's characteristic way of thinking, feeling, and behaving, and character education has as its goal the development of the expression and thought of moral goodness.

History of Character Education

One can trace the education of moral goodness back to early philosophers, such as Aristotle and Socrates. Jumping ahead to more recent times, throughout the 19th century, schools played a critical role in the education of character and were supported by similar principles of character taught by the family in the home. Early in the 20th century, however, new scientific theories, such as Darwinism and behaviorism, challenged the concepts of teaching moral goodness in the schools. Behaviorism introduced the idea that moral behavior and thought were situation-specific and not a set of generalizable qualities that one could teach or maintain over time. Still, not until the 1950s did schools reduce their focus on the education of moral principles, which left these concepts to be taught in the home. This trend remained throughout the '60s, '70s, and '80s. The '90s saw the resurgence of teaching moral thinking, feeling, and behaving through character education as one response to the increased violence and decreased humanity demonstrated by youth. Educators nationwide have begun to promote character education as a means of addressing the real or perceived moral decline of the country (Brooks & Kahn, 1993), and current public opinion polls indicate that more than 48 percent of survey respondents believe character education should be required in schools, while less than 7 percent say character education should not be part of the education curriculum (Gallup, 1999).

The high demand for character education has resulted in packaged character education kits flooding the market. Character education is integrated into the current curriculum or taught as a separate course. Schools vary in their degree of involvement with the education of moral goodness through the school curriculum and student conduct polices; however, most elementary and secondary schools in America have embraced the concepts of teaching respect, responsibility, and democratic values through social studies and civics classes. Unfortunately, as the demand for character education increases beyond its traditional place in social studies and civics classes, so, too, does the need for professional development of teachers. As Jones, Ryan, and Bohlin (1998) note, student teachers are not adequately prepared to teach character education, and the discrepancy between their preparedness and increasing public expectations is growing.

The Character Education Controversy

Even as the teaching of moral character in the schools is increasing in popularity and depth of content, the teaching of moral goodness in the classroom is not without controversy. The most controversial question surrounding character education in the schools is whether it should be taught at all. Does character education provided by schools really develop "good" character, or does the final forming of one's character lie solely within an individual?

Great numbers of philosophers, school reform agents, educators, and parents believe that children must be taught character, and although the primary source of character education is the responsibility of caregivers at home, educational institutions should not ignore the concept of teaching character (Likona, 1991). For opponents, character education remains too closely connected to religious morality. Most educators' training in moral goodness comes from their religious and civic backgrounds (Ryan, 1989), and without extensive training in the fundamentals of other religions, educators' version of character education might merely become an extension of their own belief systems. Since much of character education reflects views of human nature and is potentially influenced by and grounded in an individual educator's spirituality (Simpson, 1989) or religious beliefs, the connection between character education and religious morality is perceived as a threat to the neutrality of public education. Given the possible restriction of First Amendment rights and the lack of a clearly defined connection between character education and academic competence, many state strongly that character education does not belong in school settings.

Proponents of character education argue that the education of universal moral conduct does not interfere with the diversity of this country's religious preferences (Likona, 1991). In 1948, the United Nations addressed the content of universal morals with its Universal Declaration of Human Rights, marking the universality of life, liberty, and the pursuit of freedom, among other rights. Based on these established universal morals, educators in the '90s consistently embraced two overriding school goals of character education, respect and responsibility. The education of respect and responsibility—in behavior and thought—toward one another and toward the school community is not based on religion, advocates claim (Nucci, 1989).

Also in support of character education in the schools, Wynne and Walberg (1984) state that academic competence and character development are not mutually exclusive but are complementary learning experiences, whereby competence allows character to be demonstrated at its highest levels and character development improves academic competence. If the content of the character education program is created for the purpose of enhancing students' socio-cognitive skills, then academic competency areas may improve. Battistich, Solomon, Watson, Solomon, and Schaps (1989) demonstrate the positive impact of a character education program on the cognitive social problem-solving skills and strategies of elementary school children. In their study, children exposed to a character education program demonstrated greater critical thinking skills and were able to generalize these skills from social situations to other academic school content areas. Their thinking about challenges, obstacles, and solutions regarding interpersonal relationships was heightened by learned feelings of respect, responsibility, and empathy toward others.

Regardless of the controversy surrounding both the inclusion of character education in schools and its content, many school leaders believe that character education is critical to student education and, increasingly, to

benefits. Students make individual responses at this age, according to Kohlberg, based on rewards and punishments for their behaviors, as the following example indicates.

A preschool class of four- and five-year-olds is presented with the following scenario. Sally was playing with a new toy on her mother's new desk. The toy slipped and made a big scratch on the top of the desk. Later, Sally's mother asked her if she knew where the scratch came from. A typical classroom discussion might sound like this:

Teacher: Should Sally tell her mother she created the scratch?

Student 1:   No, she shouldn't tell.

Teacher: Why shouldn't Sally tell her mother?

Student 1:   Because she might get a spanking, or she might not be able to play on the table again, or she might have her toy taken away.

Kohlberg's second phase of moral development, the conventional stage, is commonly found in middle childhood, when students behave and think according to the moral standards society creates; therefore, students at this level base their moral action and thought on societal acceptance. Finally, the postconventional level of moral reasoning, developmentally appropriate for older students, is the stage in which personal convictions and autonomous thought dictate moral action and behavior. Traditionally, this level represents the ultimate moral character, which risks the self and popularity in favor of valuing moral principles.

All children, according to Kohlberg's theory, progress through these stages of moral development, although some students progress further and faster than others. The use of more sophisticated methods of processing information on moral dilemmas can depend on exposure to environments that support moral dialogue with individuals at adjacent but higher stages of development.

CONNECTING CHARACTER EDUCATION
TO CONFLICT RESOLUTION EDUCATION

Character education and conflict resolution education have been closely tied in many safe school plans. One connection between the two topics is that character influences how students resolve intrapersonal conflict, which, in turn, influences interpersonal conflict resolution. For instance, many character education programs promote traits of constructive interpersonal relationships, such as integrity, kindness, respect, and responsibility. Sweeney and Carruthers (1996) conceptualize character education and conflict resolution education on a continuum with the two approaches to education as anchors on each end. On one end, character education guides individuals in social and emotional development to handle interpersonal relationships better. On the other end, conflict resolution education supports positive interpersonal relationships that reinforce intrapersonal development of respect, kindness, and responsibility.

Enright (1980) finds that character education on kindness topics improved students' problem-solving skills during interpersonal conflict. Enright reports that teachers assisting students in resolving real-life interpersonal conflicts asked the students to identify what happened during the conflict, how they think what happened affected the other disputant's feelings, what else the disputants might have done to resolve the conflict, and what they would do if a similar situation occurred in the future. After 11 weeks of character education, students scored significantly higher in ability to reason about fairness than a matched class of students who did not have character education. Hence, character education and conflict resolution education might work in synchrony, with character education promoting development of intrapersonal traits and conflict resolution education developing interpersonal traits.

The California Child Development Project, funded by the Hewlett Foundation, was a longitudinal study from 1983 to 1989 to evaluate empirically the effects of a character education program on moral knowledge, skills, and attitudes of upper elementary grade students (Battistich, Solomon, Watson, & Schaps, 1997; Battistich et al., 1989; Solomon, Watson, Battistich, Schaps, Delucchi, 1996; Solomon, Watson, Delucchi, Schaps, Battistich, 1988). The original study involved three program and three comparison schools, matched in pairs on the basis of student demographics and school factors (size), then randomly assigned to a condition. The study followed a cohort of children from kindergarten through sixth grade who were exposed to a character education program throughout the years they were enrolled in the program schools. The students were predominantly middle class and White (subsequent findings included more diverse student populations). Students received education on moral content and moral processes. Results of the study strongly connect character education and skills necessary for the peaceful resolution of conflict. Compared with children not exposed to the program, participants demonstrated significantly relevant findings in four areas:

1. Classroom behavior improved, with a greater number of students demonstrating affection, cooperation, and encouragement toward one another.

2. Playground behavior improved, with students demonstrating greater concern for others.

3. Social problem-solving skills improved, with students resolving hypothetical situations with less aggressive solutions, more alternative plans, and more attention to the needs of all parties.

4. Students embraced a greater number of democratic views, with an increase in the belief that all members of a group have the right to participate in decision making.

Conflict resolution education and character education also assist with the founding of democratic thought. A democracy is government by the people who ensure a free society. All individuals must be responsible, respect the rights of individuals, and possess concern for the common good. Students' display of constructive conflict resolution strategies, such as negotiation and mediation, establishes equality among students in the classroom, an important aspect in developing individual democratic characteristics.

STRATEGIES FOR IMPLEMENTING CHARACTER EDUCATION

It is the responsibility of schools to incorporate character education through three means: curriculum, environment, and opportunities for action—CEO. CEO is the mechanism through which character education in the schools can improve students' constructive resolution of intrapersonal conflict.

Curriculum

Curricula are available for character education (see Appendix C: Resources); however, many of these programs do not include information on teaching students how to resolve intrapersonal conflict constructively. Many resources are available for educators interested in teaching specific values, such as respect and honesty, with ideas for adding this information to classroom content. Character education programs are programs implemented in elementary, middle, or high schools involving deliberate, proactive attempts to foster positive character development.

Character education programs are distinguished by a predominant emphasis in the program materials and implementation on instilling, teaching, or promoting a range of core values (described also as ethical values, moral values, virtues, character traits, or principles). Character education programs have features that overlap with those of such other program areas as social-emotional development, conflict resolution, violence prevention, social skills training, and service learning. Student outcomes of these types of character education programs include the following:

- *Understanding values:* Students' ability to recognize values and how they may affect people and actions in different situations, their understanding of ethical dilemmas, and their ability to make critical judgments about their own and other people's behavior in different situations

- *Caring about values:* The perceived importance of core values and students' opinions about how they should behave in different situations
- *Enacting values:* Behavior that displays core values (e.g., participation in community service), prosocial behavior (e.g., supporting peers), or decreased problem behavior (e.g., substance use, fighting, disciplinary referrals)

Unfortunately, little is available for educators to teach moral thought process (rather than content). Teachers can use hypothetical scenarios to help students think about moral issues. Making the link between moral thought processes and thoughts about intrapersonal and interpersonal conflict is easier with hypothetical situations rather than with curricula that teaches specific values solely. Teachers may need to select and combine a number of value content programs to address moral thought processes.

Although not clearly identified as character education, some manners education programs teach moral thought processes. For example, the Oh, My Manners! education curriculum (Kingberry Productions, 2008) uses animated characters (see Figure 3.2) to teach manners for the purposes of enhancing classroom management and improving peer interpersonal relationships. The socio-cognitively based curriculum uniquely combines concrete examples and story problem solving for the purpose of teaching skills such as cooperative turn taking, empathy, and other constructive

Figure 3.2   Manners Characters

SOURCE: Used with permission of Kingberry Productions, Inc.

behaviors for use in the classroom, hallways, and on the playground. Direct reference and student reflection of manners to conflict resolution are featured in the Oh, My Manners curriculum.

Character education should not be a separate teaching unit; like conflict resolution education, it should be infused throughout the curriculum, a component of all topics. Students should be exposed to character education concepts throughout the school and throughout the curriculum rather than as a separate course elective. Teachers should present exercises and activities that ask students to view moral and ethical dilemmas. Students need to explore, according to Kohn (1997), complex issues and recast the issues with their own experience.

Teachers can support moral character development in the following ways:

- *Expose students to real-life challenges.* Particularly useful are role-play exercises or scenarios about moral situations that involve children.
- *Involve students in resolving moral dilemmas cooperatively.* Mixing students from differing Kohlberg levels (see Figure 3.1) provides intrapersonal conflict between their moral thought processes and those of other students. Matching students so each pair's abilities are one adjacent Kohlberg level apart produces cognitive conflict and the opportunity for cognitive advancement.

Environment

The greatest impact character education might have is creating a school environment supportive of moral thought. When students perceive their school as a moral community, they are more likely to behave in moral ways (Power, Higgins, & Kohlberg, 1989). Strategies that support teaching moral thought focus on student relationships as well as staff–student relationships. School leaders should be prepared to model moral reasoning and mutual respect through nonauthoritarian relationships with students. As described earlier, in the preschool-age classroom, students were more likely to lie to mother about the origin of the scratch to avoid punishment. Authoritarian methods of teaching consistently reinforce this way of thinking. Likona (1991) outlines six elements of a moral culture in the school:

1. Moral and academic leadership from the principal
2. School discipline codes that reflect school expectations
3. School sense of community among parents, staff, and students
4. Student government run by students and guided by adults that invites democracy into the school and classroom and underscores that students do have a voice

5. Moral atmosphere of respect, fairness, and cooperation across relationships

6. Time spent on moral concerns to elevate morality

Offering Opportunities for Student Action

School leaders should be willing to provide students with opportunities to act in a morally correct manner. They can, for example, encourage service to the school and the community through adopt-a-store programs, where students pitch in to help store owners clean their parking lots, or adopt-people programs, where students develop relationships with local business owners, government officials, and seniors. Students should not be rewarded for participating in such activities; rather, these activities should be part of school expectations. Some schools require service to the community as a graduation requirement, then provide numerous opportunities for students to meet the required hours through collaborations with local youth organizations, religious organizations, and businesses.

POTENTIAL PITFALLS IN CHARACTER EDUCATION

Although the education of character is extremely popular, and many educators and parents are enthusiastic about implementing programs in the school and classroom, it is critical that school leaders address some of the following potential program pitfalls before beginning or proceeding with character education:

- *Lack of understanding of the goal of character education:* All involved need to be clear about the goal of character education programs and the desired approach to achieving the goal. If the desired goal is to teach students the process of moral thought so they can better address interpersonal conflict, programs should support the goal.
- *Inappropriate expectations for young students:* Developmental appropriateness for moral thought is extremely important. Just as fifth graders should not be expected to be capable of understanding calculus principles, second graders cannot sufficiently respond to capital punishment–level moral dilemmas.
- *Lack of program infusion into the school through curricula, environment, and opportunities for action:* School leaders should avoid naming November the Trust Month or friendliness as the virtue of the third week in October.

- *Lack of infusion of character education throughout the curriculum, from language arts to physical education classes:* Do not separate character education into a separate unit; students will then treat it as separate information and not generalize the lessons to daily life. Differentiating moral content from the curriculum is like teaching hypothesis testing separately from science principles.
- *Feeling discouragement with small, incremental changes in student behavior:* Students may not demonstrate significant changes overnight. In the California Child Development Project cited earlier in this chapter, marked changes occurred after several years.
- *Belief that rewards create "good" student behavior and punishment corrects "evil" student behavior:* A school principal once reported that students actually turned in their own clothing to the lost-and-found just to be recognized for their kindness in conducting the act. School leaders should work toward removing external rewards (candy, material goods, accolades, etc.) and help students identify internal rewards for their behavior.

SUCCESSFUL CHARACTER EDUCATION PROGRAMS

Too Good for Violence

Too Good for Violence promotes character values, social-emotional skills, and healthy beliefs in elementary and middle school students. The program includes seven lessons per grade level for elementary school (K–5) and nine lessons per grade level for middle school (Grades 6–8). All lessons are scripted and engage students through role-playing and cooperative learning games, small group activities, and classroom discussions. Students are encouraged to apply these skills to different contexts. Too Good for Violence also includes optional parental and community involvement elements.

Connect with Kids

Connect with Kids aims to promote prosocial attitudes and positive behavior of elementary (Grades 3–5) and secondary (Grades 6–12) school students by teaching core character values. Lesson plans include videos, story summaries, discussion questions, student games, and activities for both core and supplemental character traits. The classroom curriculum is reinforced by a Web site component and schoolwide and community outreach components. The program can be incorporated into an existing curriculum or used as a stand-alone program. The school or teacher decides on the number of character traits covered in each session, so the program duration may vary from one semester to an entire academic year.

Positive Action

Positive Action, a K–12 program, aims to promote character development, academic achievement, and social-emotional skills and to reduce disruptive and problem behavior. The program is based on the philosophy that you feel good about yourself when you think and do positive actions and that there is always a positive way to do everything. The curriculum includes six units; some grades have a review for a seventh unit. All lessons are scripted and use classroom discussion, role-playing, games, songs, and activity sheets or text booklets. Optional components are sitewide climate development; drug education for Grade 5 and middle school; conflict resolution; counselor, parent, and family classes; and community/coalition components.

4

Implementing Conflict Resolution Education

If we are to teach real peace in this world and if we are to carry on a real war against war, we shall have to begin with the children.

—Mahatma Gandhi (1869–1948)

THE FOURTH R: RESOLUTION

Many school leaders, keenly aware of the need to teach beyond the three Rs, now agree that a fourth R, resolution, is essential. Conflict resolution education for students of all ages is critical to creating and sustaining safer schools. Conflict resolution education is widespread in the United States and stands out as one of the most effective strategies for developing safe schools.

Conflict resolution education and violence prevention curricula are both methods useful to school leaders seeking to improve the student education area of school safety. Conflict resolution education encompasses teaching students to resolve interpersonal conflicts constructively. Its purpose is to combat all destructive forms of resolution, including violence, conflict avoidance, and conflict withdrawal, and produce more successful interpersonal interactions.

GOALS OF CONFLICT RESOLUTION EDUCATION

The primary goal of all conflict resolution education is to affect changes in students' skills, knowledge, and attitudes regarding the nature of conflict and constructive resolution of interpersonal conflict. Conflict resolution curricula provide students with the opportunity to demonstrate and improve communication and problem-solving skills through role-playing conflict situations and generating responses to hypothetical situations. Introducing students to conflict-related terms, such as *mediation, negotiation,* and *conciliation,* and improving students' methods of expressing themselves are ways in which conflict resolution curricula improve student knowledge and skills. Understanding that conflict can provide opportunities for and constructive methods of conflict resolution that produce more desirable outcomes than violent methods helps shape students' attitudes toward more prosocial behaviors.

One form of conflict resolution education involves teaching students constructive social skills. Social skills training programs often reduce the need for teachers to intervene in students' interpersonal conflict. Thus, they are extremely useful for classroom management and have resulted in significant reductions in school-related conflict and violence (Deutsch, 1993). Violence prevention curricula are a specialized form of conflict resolution education where students learn to resolve conflict without violence.

The most effective conflict resolution education appears to be a comprehensive program that includes building students' self-awareness and enhancing students' interpersonal interactions through effective communication and listening, empathy and perspective taking, and problem-solving skills.

BUILDING STUDENTS' SELF-AWARENESS

Educators who help students improve their self-awareness are increasing protective factors against youth violence. Protective factors are influences that ameliorate risk factors and promote the characteristics of resilience. Conflict resolution programs that improve student self-awareness foster youth resilience against violence and antisocial behaviors by teaching youth to control their own behaviors by making choices that satisfy their needs and building youths' sense of competency and trust in their abilities for positive human relations.

Self-Esteem

Self-esteem is a global judgment of self-worth and how well you like who you perceive yourself to be. Research on self-esteem indicates that individuals' level of self-esteem is a product of two internal judgments. According to Harter (1990), an individual experiences differences between what he or she would like to be and what the individual thinks he or she is. When that discrepancy is low, a student's self-esteem is relatively high. On the other hand, when the discrepancy is high, a student's self-esteem is low.

Self-esteem is often interrelated with social support as perceived by the individual. When one feels surrounded by individuals who are supportive and nurturing, one's self-esteem is higher than that of an individual who perceives his or her environment as hostile. Although a relatively stable construct over time, self-esteem is impacted by judgments from others. Negative labels and experiences with peers may affect a student's self-perception.

The direct connection between self-esteem and violence is controversial. Indeed, victimized students tend to be anxious and suffer from low-esteem. On the other hand, bullies who engage in violent and aggressive behaviors do not always suffer from low self-esteem. In fact, many females who engage in relational bullying have inflated levels of self-esteem. For this reason, conflict resolution education programs should be implemented in schools for purposes of promoting resiliency in victimized students and as a means to ward off the behaviors of perpetrators.

Anger Management

Identifying and managing anger are important skills for the constructive resolution of conflict. Students often related anger with power, and power-based conflict is often resolved in ways that are destructive. Anger management is a useful tool to control the outcome of conflict situations, particularly potentially violent conflict. The goal of all anger management programs should be to assist students in learning how to reduce the emotional and physiological arousal that anger causes. The program's goals should never be aimed at the impossible task of eliminating anger but rather at learning to control its effects on others and their environment.

Individuals tend to respond to anger in themselves and others through "fight" or "flight" behaviors. During conflict, students physiologically express the need to repress the feelings of anger by fleeing or ignoring a conflict situation, or they will face the conflict and address their anger through violent and aggressive behaviors. Anger management techniques allow students to express their emotions in socially acceptable ways.

Managing one's natural tendency to confront or flee anger is a critical step toward constructive conflict resolution. Anger management training emphasizes (a) identifying how the body reacts when angry, (b) an awareness of "hot buttons" in conflict situations, and (c) an understanding of how to address angry emotions. This knowledge is integral for students to be better positioned to control the outcomes of conflict situations.

Classroom Exercise: Hot Buttons

Ask students to describe situation in which they felt angry and to brainstorm about how their bodies felt when they were angry. Next, ask students to identify the outcomes of these situations. Did the angry situations always result in conflict? Peaceful resolution? What might make the difference between situations in which you are angry and the situation is resolved versus situations that go unresolved? Have the students work in pairs and instruct them to create a list of behaviors by others (exclude specific names) that make them "hot." In another column, have them identify what happens next when their "hot buttons" get pushed and they get angry. In a skills-building exercise, ask students to role-play two hot-button situations, and to create strategies for managing their anger toward improved conflict resolution.

Once students have identified their hot buttons and how they feel when angry and they understand the possible outcomes, skill building should occur around stress and relaxation techniques. According to Dahlen and Deffenbacher (2001), relaxation coping skills target both the emotional and physiological arousal associated with anger with the intent of lowering the anger arousal.

Classroom Tip

Create mandatory relaxation techniques for the classroom. Ask students to repeat the techniques often. Start the day and end the day with these techniques. For instance, teachers may have postures they ask the students to adopt as a way to calm things down. Asking the students to close their eyes and sit with their shoulders relaxed, their hands on the desk with palms facing upward, and their legs outstretched for a few minutes before beginning a lesson can relax the mood in the class. An isometric exercise includes folding both hands and pushing very hard against each hand for eight to ten seconds followed by two to three deep breathes. Another is pushing both feet against the floor while pulling up with both hands underneath the chair. The principle behind each activity is that an immediate physical action can neutralize and reduce tension created by the surge of adrenaline often present during a conflict situation.

PERSPECTIVE TAKING AND EMPATHY

A critical cornerstone of constructive conflict resolution is perspective taking, the ability to see multiple perspectives simultaneously. Perspective taking involves trying to understand how others feel about a situation and sensing or understanding the thoughts and feelings of others, important skills for students to possess for the peaceful resolution of conflict situations. Knowledge of active listening vocabulary and use of active listening skills blend well with teaching individuals perspective taking and the benefits of perspective-taking skills in daily interpersonal interactions. The inability to communicate effectively greatly inhibits one's ability to take the perspective of others and think critically. Effective communicators are more likely to identify and understand multiple points of view. During conflict situations, individuals opposing each other naturally hold different views on the topic at issue. When conflict escalates, anger escalates, and communication tends to be less interactive. If disputants can effectively use good communication strategies—active listening and *I* messages—they might fill in gaps in information regarding the conflict and perhaps see the other person's point of view. Although effective communication might not change the minds of the disputants, it offers them an opportunity to see how the other individual views the conflict and, hence, promotes perspective taking. Students practice perspective-taking skills through role-playing and critical-thinking exercises.

Researchers indicate that sophisticated perspective-taking skills are related to a variety of social skills, including constructive problem-solving abilities (Bosworth, Espelage, & Dubay, 1998). Students with sophisticated perspective-taking skills are better problem solvers and are more likely to generate sophisticated methods of handling difficult social situations (Marsh, Serafica, & Barenboim, 1981). Therefore, children with better affective perspective-taking skills are often more capable of handling everyday social conflict in constructive ways.

Perspective-taking skills are developmentally determined and learned over time. Children younger than seven years of age are believed to have only a limited ability to understand what other people think and feel (Piaget, 1932). For instance, when adults ask a child, "How do you think Johnny feels when you do that?" they often receive an unsatisfactory response. Many classic cognitive psychologists, such as Piaget, believe that children younger than seven have only a limited cognitive capability to understand how Johnny feels. This limitation plays a significant role in children's ability to generate and select conflict resolution strategies equitable to both parties.

Gradually, children become more conscious of the fact that others can interpret the same event in different ways and become able to step into another person's shoes: a shift occurs between the ages of five and seven, with full recognition occurring after age seven. At this time, children are cognitively capable of resolving conflict in a manner mutually beneficial to the disputants. During the middle childhood years, Grades 2 through 6, conflict resolution education plays a significant role in supporting cognitive advancements in perspective taking and provides students with opportunities to practice their budding ability to take others' perspectives.

One way of viewing the connection between cognitive capabilities and perspective taking and conflict resolution strategy selection is found in the work of Robert Selman (Selman, 1980, 1981; Selman, Jaquette, & Bruss-Saunders, 1979). A developmental psychologist, Selman theorizes that individuals progress through qualitatively different stages of perspective-taking abilities and these stages influence interpersonal negotiation skills. Individuals may interpret social conflict in an egocentric/undifferentiated manner (Level 0), and resolved conflicts through physically aggressive and impulsive behaviors. At Level 1, individuals examine conflictual inter-actions in a subjective and unilateral manner, by weighing their needs over those of the other conflict participants. At Level 2, children identify conflict as occurring to two participants with equal rights in the situation. Level 3 consists of behaviors that are mutually beneficial to both disputants, truly collaborative behavior and concern for the relation-ship, the highest level of interpersonal understanding. As individuals progress developmentally, interpersonal nego-tiation abilities are augmented, not replaced. In other words, adults are cog-nitively capable of using Level 0, 1, 2, and 3 strategies during conflict, while children ages three to nine are cogni-tively capable of Levels 0 and 1.

An adaptation of Selman's (1981) interpersonal negotiation strategy model appears in Figure 4.1. As the figure depicts, children in Levels 0 and 1 have limited ability to understand the perspectives of others. This limitation causes students to identify problems inaccurately, inhibits appropriate identification of feelings of disputants, interferes with the genera-tion of multiple and sophisticated strategies for the resolution of the conflict, and results in conflict resolution strategies that favor one participant over another.

Recognition of the cognitive limitations of young students may suggest to some that conflict resolution education does not benefit this age group, and true collaboration and negotiation is not possible before age ten. However, it is important to appreciate that most students are cognitively capable of behaving in constructive ways during conflict but often choose to behave in a less sophisticated manner due to a number of factors, includ-ing past experiences that reinforce certain functioning levels. For example, secondary students are cognitively capable of demonstrating a Level 3 response to a conflict situation. However, during conflict that occurs in the home, they may have been exposed only to Level 1, with parents telling their children how to resolve the conflict. For example, a student and an older sib-ling are fighting over the television remote control. A parent comes in and tells the older sibling to give the remote to the younger sibling. For the student, this parent model reinforces use of Level 1 conflict resolution because as the younger sibling, he or she got his way. One objective of perspective-taking education is to reinforce conflict resolution techniques that more accurately

Figure 4.1   Interpersonal Negotiation Strategy

The following is an adaptation of Robert Selman's (1981) model of interpersonal negotiation. The age ranges are approximate and not absolute. The levels listed are guidelines of cognitive capability and corresponding socio-cognitive expectations during conflict. They suggest more of a continuum rather than absolute, mutually exclusive categories of thinking. Differences in expectations may occur, just as some flexibility of cognitive capabilities of young children occur.

Level 0: Approximate Ages 3–6 Years

Profound egocentrism marks Level 0. Children are unable to understand or appreciate fully the motivations and feelings of others. They use common conflict resolution strategies to protect the self but do not seek to maintain friendships. Conflict resolution strategies of Level 0 include the following:

- *Aggression*—Physical fighting, yelling, making the other person feel bad
- *Avoidance/withdrawal*—Running away, pretending nothing is wrong

Level 1: Approximate Ages 4–9 Years

Level 1 is an improvement over Level 0 in perspective-taking skills, yet this level is still marked by inability to understand or appreciate fully the motivations and feelings of others. Children at this developmental level do not believe that others' perspectives are of equal importance. Typically, they report that their own perspectives have greater value than other perspectives. Decisions are not based on continuing friendships. Common conflict resolution strategies demonstrated by children in this level include the following:

- *Giving in*—Letting others have their way
- *Standing one's ground*—"I'm right: they're wrong."

Level 2: Approximate Ages 7–12 Years

At Level 2, children have the ability to understand and appreciate the motivations and feelings of others; however, they are unable to resolve conflict situations by themselves and require third-party intervention. Common conflict resolution strategies exhibited at this level include the following:

- *Appealing to an authority*—Asking parents or teachers to decide a conflict, flipping a coin
- *Compromise*—Taking turns, sharing

Level 3: Approximate Ages 10–Adult

At Level 3, individuals have the ability to understand and appreciate the motivations and feelings of others. They have a desire to maintain a relationship with the disputing partner and do not require third-party intervention. Common conflict resolution strategies demonstrated at this level include the following:

- *Collaboration*—Negotiation, creating solutions that accommodate needs of both disputants

reflect the students' cognitive capability. Once students behave in a developmentally appropriate fashion, conflict resolution education facilitates students' positive experiences with more sophisticated levels of interpersonal understanding and more constructive methods of conflict resolution.

The Selman model can help school leaders define developmentally appropriate curricula for students, as well as set goals for students with lower levels of perspective-taking ability. Educators should pair students in cooperative learning groups with students of varying levels of perspective-taking abilities. Pairing students in Level 3 with those in Level 1 results in significant improvements in conflict resolution strategy selection by the Level 1 students. Interestingly, the Level 3 students do not resort to the lower levels of functioning; rather, they tend to bring up the other students, whose lower levels of functioning are unacceptable to them.

ENHANCING STUDENTS' INTERPERSONAL INTERACTIONS

Communication Skills

Teaching students to communicate effectively with each other is an important goal of all conflict resolution education programs (Sweeney & Carruthers, 1996), as one of the greatest causes of conflict is poor communication and the inability to express oneself accurately and listen carefully to others. Effective communication skills are necessary to resolve conflict constructively. Teaching active listening skills and the use of *I* messages is the first step in conflict resolution education and more peaceful classrooms and safer schools.

Active Listening Techniques

The use of active listening techniques plays a critical role in the constructive resolution of interpersonal conflict. Active listening requires the disputants to take turns speaking and listening, which often diffuses much of the anger accompanying the conflict while helping the disputing pair resolve the conflict through constructive methods of resolution rather than through destructive methods, such as violence. Conflict often arises because of two communication problems: (1) individuals lack important information regarding a situation or a disputant's feelings or (2) individuals possess inaccurate information regarding the situation or the other disputant's feelings. Successful active listening allows disputing students to fill in gaps in their knowledge regarding the situation or each other's feelings. Active listening techniques encourage positive dialogue, and as one element of that dialogue, the speaker must feel that the listener is interested in what he or she is saying and is willing to participate in the dialogue. Through words and nonverbal communication, students learn to create a safe environment for a speaker.

The instruction of active listening skills is a twofold process. Students must learn the definitions of the active listening terms, then have opportunities to practice the skills associated with active listening. Role-play is an effective technique for teaching the active listening vocabulary and allowing students to practice effective communication behaviors. Teachers should first model the skills a number of times in the role of listener while students play the role of speaker. To demonstrate the effectiveness of active listening techniques in conflict resolution, teachers can have students role-play a conflict using active listening skills and compare it with the identical conflict when the disputants do not use the techniques. Homework assignments related to active listening skills might ask students to use these skills with parents and other siblings and identify any unusual outcomes. Or students can watch television and note the number of times characters do or do not use active listening skills. Because active listening requires quite a bit of practice, teachers should provide numerous opportunities for students to use these skills across the curriculum. According to Lantieri and Patti (1996), active listening skills consist of six important techniques: paraphrasing, clarification, reflection, encouragement, validation, and summary (see also Figure 4.2).

Figure 4.2   Active Listening Skills Techniques

Teaching the six-step process of active listening skills (Lantieri & Patti, 1996) is an important first step in educating students about constructive conflict resolution skills and encouraging conflict resolution knowledge.

- *Paraphrasing:* Listeners repeat back what the speaker has said as closely as possible.
- *Clarification:* Listeners ask questions of the speaker about what the speaker has said during the conversation to support accurate paraphrasing.
- *Reflection:* Listeners repeat back the speaker's feelings; this is in contrast to paraphrasing, in which the listener repeats facts.
- *Encouragement:* Listeners use phrases and body language to help the speaker continue.
- *Validation:* Listeners use phrases and body language to let the speaker know that what he or she is saying is important.
- *Summary:* Listeners wrap up the discussion by using paraphrasing and reflection to present their understanding of the points the speaker made.

Paraphrasing

Conflict resolution education teaches students the common skill of paraphrasing, which involves listening to a partner, then repeating back the information to demonstrate understanding. Some simple paraphrasing exercises ask students to talk in pairs about summer vacation plans or an impending store purchase with one student being the listener and the other the speaker. When the speaker finishes the description, the listener paraphrases the partner's speech. Paraphrasing is often difficult for those new to the technique, as it can feel artificial. Initially, students often "parrot," repeating the exact words of the speaker. But the skill of paraphrasing improves with practice and continued exposure to the technique.

Clarification

Clarification is an active listening technique that supports paraphrasing because it is a means of gathering information during communication. In most cases, clarification requires the listener to ask open-ended questions of the speaker that help the listener understand both the speaker's message and the speaker's thinking about the message. Examples of the technique of clarification include the following: "How did you feel when that happened?" "Tell me more about your planned vacation," and "How often do you vacation in this spot?" When two disputants use clarification, it demonstrates interest in the telling of each "side" of the conflict, and it ensures that both parties understand statements made. Conflict resolution education emphasizes not only when and why to use the clarification technique but also how not to use the techniques. Too much clarification can make the speaker uncomfortable, as can too little clarification.

Reflection

Reflection is similar to paraphrasing, except reflection involves a restatement of feelings instead of facts. Listeners try to iterate the partner's feelings about the topic through such statements as "It seems you are pretty excited about the trip," or "It sounds like you are angry that student cut in front of you in line." Use of reflection is particularly important during conflict situations because it demonstrates that the listener has "read between the lines" in determining an emotional component to the story. Conflict resolution education teaches students to identify and echo accurately feelings expressed during communication sessions.

Encouragement and Validation

Through encouragement and validation, listeners demonstrate that they are willing to listen and that they acknowledge the importance of the discussion. Listeners exhibit the skill of encouragement and validation with phrases such as "I would like to hear more," "Tell me more," and "Go ahead, I'm listening." Nonverbal communication methods are another way listeners demonstrate encouragement and validation. Nonverbal communication includes physical gestures, such as nodding or maintaining eye contact, that demonstrate that the listener is interested in continuing the discussion with the speaker.

Summary

When summarizing, the listener wraps up the conversation, putting together all of the information garnered through the other techniques, particularly paraphrasing, clarification, and reflection. Summarizing differs from paraphrasing, because paraphrasing involves mostly factual information and is conducted throughout the interaction. An accurate summary that correctly identifies the speaker's feelings is particularly reinforcing for young people. Summarizing helps disputants clearly define the issue of the conflict and their feelings associated with the conflict. All speakers desire to be "heard." The summary technique demonstrates that the speaker was heard and encourages the speaker to use the technique as the listener.

Classroom Tip

Ask pairs of students to take turns practicing the active listening skills. One at a time, students should discuss Topic 1 for three minutes. Next, students switch, and the listener hears his or her partner on Topic 1 for three minutes. Proceed through the additional two topics. Debriefing questions include (a) Was it easier to talk or listen? (b) How did you know your partner was listening? (c) How did the active listening skills change, given the nature of the topic (least personal to more personal topics). Topics are (1) favorite hobby or sport, (2) favorite toy (from childhood), and (3) life-changing event.

I *Messages*

A critical component of effective communication skills in conflict resolution education, *I* messages are usually taught after active listening skills. During heated interpersonal conflicts, people often lose focus of the main issues underlying the conflict. When anger is great, it is common to hear *you* statements: "You always do _____!" "You never do ____!" or "You are such a ___!" *You* statements tend to heighten anger among conflict participants. *I* messages focus on the speaker's feelings and highlight the source of these feelings.

I messages traditionally possess at least three useful components (Gordon, 1979), and many agree that a fourth component is also an important aspect for constructive conflict resolutions (Girard & Koch, 1996). These messages open with (1) a statement of the speaker's feelings ("I feel _____") followed by (2) the behavior that is the source of the feelings ("when you _____."). For instance, one might make the statement "I feel frustrated [a specific emotion] when you leave the locker door unlocked [a specific behavior of the other individual]. *I* messages continue with (3) the reason this behavior affects the speaker ("because _____") and can finish with (4) a realistic behavior the listener might engage in to alleviate the emotion ("I would like it if you _____."). So the complete statement might be "I feel frustrated when you leave the locker door unlocked because I keep a lot of expensive items in the locker. I would like you to try to remember to lock the locker." Often, *I* messages do not include the suggestion for a follow-up behavior but pass the opportunity and responsibility to the listener to provide a suggestion to change the behavior discussed.

Conflict resolution education focuses on helping students identify and describe their feelings accurately and appropriately. For example, most students say, "I'm mad," when they might really feel frustrated or hurt or anxious. Emotion identification helps sculpt the *I* message to have greater meaning for both the speaker and the listener. Students also learn how to describe the behavior of another person in a nonjudgmental way. For instance, the statement "I feel frustrated when you are inconsiderate," is not only more ambiguous but is more derogatory than the statement "I feel frustrated when you leave the locker door unlocked." In addition, the first statement is more difficult to follow with a suggestion for a behavior to address the concern, and it is less likely to be received positively and with a desire to change. *I* messages are the cornerstone for educating students on how to be assertive in conflict situations.

Assertiveness

When you are assertive, you are able to do the following:

- Express and communicate your feelings accurately.
- Ask for things you want.
- Say no to things you do not want.
- Have the opportunity to have your needs and wants met.
- Attain the respect of others.

> Assertiveness is when an individual stands up for his or her own rights in a situation without violating the rights of another individual. Assertiveness is a manner of behaving that communicates respect for others as well as commands respect for you.

Assertiveness is one strategy with which students can do something about resolving conflicts rather than just talking about them. Assertiveness is dissimilar from both aggressiveness and passivity. According to Baer (1976), aggressiveness violates the rights of another person, while passive responses disregard the individual's own rights but meet the needs of the other disputant. Assertive behavior provides a win-win solution for both individuals (Studer, 2000).

Assertiveness training is especially useful to educate victimized students on how to interact more effectively with bullies. Training also enhances witnesses' intervention skills. The assertive student is often resistant to manipulation by the bully and resistant to the bully's aggressive tendencies (Barton, 2006). As well, assertiveness training enhances witnesses' skills so that they defend the victimized student and/or challenge the bullying behavior. Goals of assertiveness training include teaching children (a) how to make assertive statements, including *I* messages, (b) how to resist manipulations and perceived threats associated with bullying and other aggressive behavior, (c) how to respond to aggressive and destructive behavior, and (d) how to enlist the support of bystanders.

Student Exercise

Learning Objectives

- Provide students with an opportunity to practice assertive statements.
- Teach students verbal and nonverbal cues associated with assertiveness.

Have students read the following scenario about Jimmi. With students working in small groups, ask them to create as many *I* statements as possible that Jimmi could use to express his frustration to the classmates in his group. Using video equipment, tape students as they role-play the situation and their generated *I* statements.

Scenario

Jimmi is a sixth-grade student. His grades in the first semester of school were excellent, but recently, he has been less motivated and interested in his studies. Jimmi has been working on a group project with four other classmates that is a significant part of his grade. At first, he liked working with his group, even though none of the other group members were his friend. Things started to go poorly when he was given the task of recording the results of the group experiments. His group mates fooled around a lot, and Jimmi didn't know when the group was actually following the assignment or just messing around with the materials. He wasn't able to keep up, which penalized the group with wrong answers and creating homework for the group, who couldn't complete the assignment in class. His grades were falling, and the group members were always picking on him. Jimmi became frustrated and wanted to give up!

After completing the videotaping, review the tape with students and ask them to list the verbal and nonverbal cues associated with assertiveness. Ask students to reflect on how they look and sound when role-playing assertive statements.

Discuss the following:

- How does assertiveness look?
- What tone of voice is most effective when being assertive?
- How do others react when one is assertive?

Constructive Conflict Resolution Strategies

Conflict resolution education focuses on teaching constructive methods of conflict resolution, such as negotiation and collaboration. Conflict resolution programs introduce the concept of constructive conflict resolution by defining and describing win-win situations. Win-win resolutions occur when both disputants benefit from the resolution of the conflict. As in the Selman model, less sophisticated methods of conflict resolution result in one disputant winning and one losing. For example, two disputants have a conflict over a ball. At Levels 0 or 1, one disputant would either aggress against the other disputant to get the ball or withdraw from the conflict and give up the ball. At a more sophisticated level, such as Level 2, the disputants would create a win-win situation so that both achieve something from the conflict: they might compromise and play with the ball together. In many schools, educators use cooperative learning activities to introduce the concepts of constructive conflict resolution (Johnson, Johnson, Dudley, & Burnett, 1992). Deutsch (1993) draws the parallel between teaching win-win solutions and cooperative learning because of several shared learning components, including positive interdependence, face-to-face interactions, and individual accountability.

The positive interdependence associated with cooperative learning sessions is also critical when generating numerous solutions to conflict situations and creating mutually beneficial, win-win solutions. As in successful collaborative interactions, the success of the activity depends on the involvement of all participants. Win-win solutions are possible only when all individuals involved contribute to the beneficial outcome of the conflict. Collaborative learning sessions are hindered by the lack of cooperation of one member, just as win-win solutions are nearly impossible to develop without the full involvement of conflict participants. Educators must teach the differences between needs and positions in a conflict situation. A position is characterized by a person's perception of what he or she wants, while needs are the unmet physical and psychological requirements that underlie most conflicts. For example, two siblings are fighting over the last box of Cracker Jack. They continue to fight because they both want the box; in other words, they have the same position. Through the use of effective communication skills, the two figure out that they have different needs. One sibling needs the Cracker Jack for a snack, while the other sibling just wants the toy surprise.

Also similar to cooperative learning experiences, win-win training emphasizes individual accountability in the outcome of the process. Students learning about negotiation of win-win situations come to appreciate that they must adhere to the conflict agreement for the disputants to realize the win-win benefits.

THE NATURE OF CONFLICT: THEORETICAL BACKGROUND

According to Levy (1989), conflict resolution principles and practices must cover both the theoretical and practical nature of conflict and conflict resolution. Behavioral psychology defines *conflict* as naturally occurring behavior that can never be eliminated from human nature. Destructive methods of conflict resolution are learned and, therefore, according to behaviorists, can be unlearned (Skinner, 1974). As in other areas of behavior, selection of certain conflict resolution strategies is the result of reinforcement and punishment. Conflict resolution education, according to behaviorists, involves reinforcing desired behaviors of constructive conflict resolution and effective communication while punishing violence and ineffective communication strategies.

Cognitive theorists describe changes in thought that occur as a result of conflict resolution education. They view individuals as possessing a conflict cycle that forms a closed feedback loop system and conflict resolution education as serving as a mechanism for reforming the feedback system. For instance, Sadalla, Henriquez, and Holmberg (1987) describe a conflict cycle that consists of a set of beliefs about a conflict. An individual's response to a conflict depends on this set of beliefs, and the consequences of the response revert the person back to the set of beliefs. Cognitive theorists believe that conflict resolution education interferes with the set of beliefs surrounding a conflict, which, in turn, interferes with a display of negative responses.

For example, every morning before school begins, the principal of the high school has to tell a group of seniors who congregate in front of the door to move away and allow other students to enter the school. Frustrated with repeating this ritual every morning, the principal frequently shouts at the students to move, sometimes sending several of the students to his office for detention. In relation to the feedback loop system, the principal has a particular set of beliefs surrounding the conflict with the group of seniors. The group responds to his shouting and authoritarian behavior, which reinforces the principal's belief systems related to the resolution of the conflict. However, if conflict resolution education presents the principal with alternative methods of resolving the dispute, he might forego punitive behaviors, such as shouting and detentions, and attempt to discuss options with the students so they contribute to the solution. When the students aren't presented with the expected punishment, their beliefs about the conflictual situation will change as well and, in turn, affect their behavior.

Finally, the humanistic approach to human development plays a critical role in conflict resolution education. According to Maslow (1968), students' ability to achieve self-actualization is based on the successful realization of concepts such as belongingness, affiliation, self-love, and perceived security. Conflict resolution education supports the potential for self-actualization by teaching students methods for resolving conflicts related to belongingness, affiliations, and other areas through win-win methods. Emphasizing and identifying needs rather than positions during conflicts more likely produces win-win resolutions.

APPROACHES TO CONFLICT RESOLUTION EDUCATION

Conflict resolution education can be taught at any grade level. Traditionally, principles of peace education and prosocial skills are emphasized in the early childhood grades, while conflict resolution and violence prevention curricula are used in upper-elementary and secondary grades.

K–12 educators frequently use two mechanisms for teaching violence prevention curricula. In the *process curriculum approach,* they use a specific time of class to teach conflict resolution education from a standardized curriculum, or they teach a separate course in conflict resolution education. The *curriculum infusion approach* involves integrating concepts of conflict resolution education throughout the existing curriculum. Lessons expose students to effective communication, perspective taking, and generating constructive resolution strategies in history, science, and even math class. Selection of the process or infusion approach depends on the outcome of the school safety team assessment. Often, schools employ a combination of the two methods, by exposing students to a standardized curriculum in addition to infusing conflict resolution lessons in other course work. A table outlining the advantages and disadvantages of the two methods appears in Figure 4.3.

Peer mediation programming is another method of providing students with constructive conflict resolution information. Peer mediation programs train a select number of school students to learn principles of conflict resolution education (see Chapter 5). The advantage of the process and infusion method over special initiatives, such as peer mediation, is that constructive conflict resolution education reaches greater numbers of students.

Figure 4.3   Process Versus Infusion Approach to Conflict Resolution Education

Effectiveness

Process approach: Standardized curriculum is often evaluated for effectiveness. Many of the standardized curriculum sets have been evaluated previously in classroom settings, providing some sense of assurance to school leaders that buying and using the products will effect changes.

Infusion approach: Little empirical evidence supports effectiveness.

Standardized Program

Process approach: Standardized curriculum provides some support for standardized instruction. Purchase of these products, with their activities, videos, and objectives, provides some sense that all participating teachers are teaching the same material in the same fashion. Everyone speaks the same language and is exposed to the same information.

Infusion approach: There is little standardization. Students receive a wide variety of conflict resolution education.

Appropriateness of Materials

Process approach: Materials might not be appropriate for all students. Most schools end up mixing and matching curriculum materials to fit their student populations. A program that provides a lot of instruction on responding to potentially violent situations in the home and to and from school might not be appropriate for schools whose students don't encounter a great deal of violence but need instruction on bullying.

Infusion approach: Teacher-created materials meet student and school needs.

Demands on Teaching Staff

Process approach: Professional development is required for greater program success, but with training, teachers find the prepackaged curriculum materials easy to use. Exercises and ancillary materials are available. Most programs have suggested discussion questions, exercises, homework, and follow-up work. Lesson plans are essentially created for the teacher. They often contain videos and posters for use in the classroom.

Infusion approach: Teaching staff must generate exercises and ancillary materials. Professional development might be necessary.

Cost

Process approach: Can be costly. Materials need to be purchased, and adequate training for use is required.

Infusion approach: Is less costly than process approach. Teachers create own lessons involving conflict resolution principles.

Time Requirements

Process approach: Involves time constraints, as teachers must add lessons. Often adds 25 to 30 minutes each week.

Infusion approach: Involves fewer time constraints, as teachers infuse exercises into current curriculum.

Process Approach

Teachers who use a specific time, a distinct curriculum, or a daily lesson on social skill principles are using the process approach to conflict resolution education. Numerous classroom resources are available to reshape student problem-solving skills (Kreidler, 1994; San Francisco Community Board Program, 1992) or their communication, cooperation, and consensus-building skills (Bodine, Crawford, & Schrumpf, 1994). Standardized programs in the process approach often provide educators with user-friendly exercises and ready-made lesson plans, manuals, student handouts, and other useful classroom material, including videotapes. The Program for Young Negotiators (PYN), based on the Harvard Negotiation Project (www.pon.harvard.edu), is representative of the process approach whereby students receive instruction in negotiation skills through a well-formed curriculum. The Second Step program (Committee for Children) offers assistance with teaching students anger management and constructive decision making using structured activities.

Curriculum Infusion Approach

Curriculum infusion involves incorporating conflict resolution principles throughout the current curriculum, such as into daily lesson plans and classroom management techniques. Core subject areas, such as language arts, science, and math, support opportunities to teach lessons on perspective taking, communication, and constructive conflict resolution. Even in schools that use the process approach, educators should be encouraged to infuse conflict resolution education throughout their current lesson plans. Curriculum infusion techniques reduce costs associated with purchasing multiple programs to fit the needs of students. In addition, these techniques help students recognize that conflict resolution skills are life skills and that students can apply them to every subject in school. Buy-in by secondary students is much greater with curriculum infusion techniques as opposed to the "Take out your workbooks. It's time to learn to be nice" programming. Because students learn through teachers' traditional lesson plans, conflict resolution education principles become more applicable to students' daily lives, and their use across multiple courses reinforces student learning.

A list of suggestions for curriculum infusion appears below; however, the possibilities for educators are limitless. All the suggested activities help improve students' skills in, knowledge of, and attitude toward effective communication, perspective taking, and conflict resolution strategies.

Language Arts

- Have students read literature and create new endings based on constructive conflict resolution methods. Nursery rhymes and fairy tales are excellent tools for helping to teach young students conflict resolution and cooperation skills. For example, discuss how Jack and Jill could work together to achieve their goal of "fetching a pail of water." Could Cinderella have used conflict resolution techniques with her stepmother and stepsisters?
- Have students rewrite stories from difference characters' perspectives. Lead students off with *True Story of the Three Little Pigs by A. Wolf* (Scieszka, 1989), the story of the three little pigs as told from the wolf's point of view.
- Have students create journals of conflicts in their lives and the lives of others. How were these solved, and what might have been the outcomes if the solutions had been different?
- Have students watch television and read the newspapers to record destructive methods of conflict resolution. Have them think about alternative solutions and how these solutions might impact future stories and television story lines.
- Have students practice communication skills at home and keep records of conversation outcomes. Students may want to keep a tally of the number of times each family member uses one of the six processes of active listening or *I* messages. When students practice these skills with family members, they should record how family members reacted to the changes in communication patterns.
- Ask students to tell a story, myth, or legend that indirectly portrays the nature of a conflict they are experiencing. For younger children, modified fairy tales are used. Stories should paint a picture of what could happen if the conflict does not end.

History and Geography

- Have students study international and domestic conflicts and offer possible constructive conflict resolution strategies. How might the world be different? It is important for students to understand the mind-set of individuals from other countries in this lesson. Have students role-play diplomats of foreign countries during an international conflict. Have students identify their country's needs and provide opportunities for the students to try to negotiate win-win solutions.
- Identify cultural barriers to communication and discuss how to overcome them.
- Study the historical context of war and policy relating to conflictual relationships.
- Discuss how different presidents dealt with conflict.
- Have students write to pen pals in other countries or states for perspective-taking and communication practice. (Try to hook up with a classroom in a state and school with a student population very different from that of your classroom.) Have students think about active listening skills and determine how often they need to use clarifying, paraphrasing, and reflection in their letters. Also, e-mail pen pals are great for thinking about the importance of nonverbal communication during discussions. For instance, would face-to-face conversations provide more information or less?

Math

- Have students create diagrams, such as bar graphs and pie charts, of statistics on incidents of violence among adolescents in the state or in the school before program intervention and after intervention. Math teachers who conduct this exercise with secondary students resistant to conflict resolution education report a twofold effect: it provides practical applications of math principles, and students who are skeptical about the relevance of teaching conflict resolution or falsely perceive their environment as "totally safe" are faced with contradictory information.
- In cooperative learning sessions, highlight the principles of win-win negotiations using math problems.
- Have students describe pictures composed of geometric shapes to students unable to see the original picture to highlight the importance of precise and accurate communication.

Music and Art

- Have students clap out of sync. Gradually, students will begin clapping in collaboration with one another. Discuss synchrony versus disharmony.

- Have students identify conflict colors and peace colors. For example, red is often associated with anger and bloodshed, while blue is associated with calmness and tranquility. Teachers can use the color wheel to have students think about individual perceptions of hot versus cool colors and what it takes to make a hot color cooler; for example, red plus white produces pink. Have students discuss what behaviors make them "red" and how they can become "pink."
- Have students view and describe three-dimensional art from various angles to highlight perspective taking, then have them compare descriptions.
- Use pointillist painters, such as Seraut, or mosaics to discuss the harmony of colors in creating whole pictures and perspective taking. Discuss how, through active listening skills, students can fill gaps of information regarding a conflict situation and how, by viewing the situation in its entirety, they are more likely to reach a harmonious outcome. The same is true of Seurat's work: individual dots of paint don't "say" much to the person viewing the piece, yet when the dots are placed together in a meaningful way, the viewer sees a completed picture.
- Assign secondary students different handheld instruments. Blindfold them and require them to find a partner with the identical instrument, using only their communication skills. (Have elementary-age students draw 3 × 5 inch cards on which the name of any instrument is printed and eliminate the blindfolds.) Students can ask any question about an instrument other than "What instrument do you have?" For example, they may ask "Does your instrument require two hands to play?" or "Does your instrument have strings?"
- Have students create drawings that reflect peace through art. Highlight the work throughout the school during the year. (Do not make the drawings part of a competition.)

PROFESSIONAL DEVELOPMENT REQUIREMENTS OF CONFLICT RESOLUTION EDUCATION

Implementation of conflict resolution education requires some professional development for school faculty. Depending on the type of programs schools select, professional development needs, however, can be minimal. For instance, when implementing conflict resolution education through the process approach, school leaders may select and purchase materials from a manufacturer who provides complete lesson plans and activities, and the use of such comprehensive materials might not require a great deal of teacher education.

Before implementing conflict resolution education, schools should consider the teacher education requirements. For the process approach, all staff members should attend at least a one-day workshop outlining the concepts of communication, perspective taking, constructive problem solving, and administration of the selected materials. Conducted through the offices of student services, curriculum and professional development, or an outside consultant, the workshop should also cover general topics regarding conflict, such as potential academic and behavioral benefits of the program. Many manufacturers of standardized curriculum offer "train-the-trainer" sessions for educators. These sessions might take place at the school or off-site. Because it is usually very expensive for manufacturers to send trainers to the school site, a more economical solution is for schools to send several persons to receive training off-site. These staff members return to the school and train the remaining staff.

With the infusion approach, the teaching staff adapts current lesson plans to add educational objectives of improving communication, perspective-taking, and problem-solving skills. The preferred method for assisting teachers with the infusion approach is to provide at least a one-day workshop outlining the principles of constructive conflict resolution, including communication skills vocabulary and behaviors, perspective taking, and win-win problem solving. For half of the session, teachers brainstorm methods for infusing these lessons into their current classroom objectives. A trained consultant experienced in the curriculum infusion model should lead this brainstorming session. As a follow-up, teachers should reconvene during the semester to share successful infusion materials and applications.

INVOLVING FAMILY MEMBERS IN CONFLICT RESOLUTION EDUCATION

It is important to build family–school partnerships when implementing conflict resolution education programs in the school and classroom. Students exposed to constructive forms of conflict resolution in the home as well as school are more likely to demonstrate long-term behavioral and cognitive changes than children presented with mixed or different strategies in the home and school. Some options for family programs and partnerships to use to improve the teaching of constructive conflict resolution in the school follow:

- Develop family conflict management training opportunities. Provide educational opportunities for family members on topics such as communication, coping with anger and stress, constructive conflict resolution, and even appropriate parenting practices. Safety team members, school professional staff (such as counselors), or outside consultants can present these programs.

- Develop family/parent nights offering fun yet educational programs dealing with conflict resolution education. Students might present skits involving their skills with and knowledge of constructive conflict resolution, or schools might sponsor a family songfest, complete with peace and multicultural songs. Some organizations, such as Second Step, offer schools that use their program information on organizing and promoting successful family involvement evenings.
- Develop school events that highlight student work associated with conflict resolution education. Display peace art, writing, or other academic work for a school event that family members attend.
- Develop parent or guardian curriculum evenings and have teachers and students talk about the conflict resolution curriculum, goals of the program, and progress during the school year.

MODELS OF EFFECTIVE CONFLICT RESOLUTION EDUCATION PROGRAMS

This section highlights some examples of conflict resolution education and violence prevention programs that show some promise.

Second Step Program

The Second Step violence prevention program of Seattle, Washington, targets children in Grades 1 through 3, although curriculum is available for students through Grade 8. Second Step, created by the Committee for Children, has 30 lesson activities and teaching modules in areas of decreasing aggressive behavior; increasing prosocial behavior; and improving empathy, anger management, and problem-solving skills. Second Step has been rigorously evaluated and has demonstrated that students exposed to the program engage in fewer aggressive behaviors and more positive behaviors on the playground and in the lunchroom than students in a control group. A longitudinal design has provided some evidence that long-term positive benefits accrue to students exposed to the curriculum (Grossman et al., 1997).

PeaceBuilders

The PeaceBuilders program closely resembles a curriculum infusion model. A schoolwide violence prevention program for students in Grades K–5, it is currently operating in nearly 400 schools across the United States. PeaceBuilders' goal is to promote prosocial behavior among children and staff, enhance social competence among students, and reduce aggressive behavior. Children are taught five simple principles: (1) praise people, (2) avoid put-downs, (3) find wise people as advisers and friends,

(4) notice and correct the hurts they cause, and (5) right the wrongs they exhibit. Preliminary evaluation of the program demonstrates teacher-reported increases in social competence and a reduction in aggressive behavior (Flannery, Huff, & Manos, 1996). The Centers for Disease Control and Prevention is funding a six-year longitudinal evaluation study of the program.

Project ACHIEVE

Project ACHIEVE, a schoolwide prevention and intervention program that targets elementary school students who are academically and socially at risk, is designed to address academic and behavioral problems. The program teaches students' social skills, problem-solving skills, and anger management techniques to reduce acts of aggression and violence. More than 20 sites across the country use Project ACHIEVE. Knoff and Batsche (1995), developers of the program, report that in one school district, the program has resulted in a decrease of suspension rates in the first three years of programming from 11 percent in Year 1 to 3 percent in Year 3. Schools also report a decrease of 28 percent in total disciplinary referrals to the principal's office.

Program for Young Negotiators (PYN)

PYN aims to build the capacity of young people, as well as those who educate and care for them, for constructive conflict resolution skills through teaching negotiation skills. Founded in 1993, PYN has received numerous awards, including an honorable mention from the Boston Plan of Excellence in the Public Schools. Preliminary evaluation demonstrates significant positive results in changing student behavior, knowledge, and attitude toward constructive conflict resolution.

Resolving Conflict Creatively Program

Educators for Social Responsibility disseminate the Resolving Conflict Creatively program. The K–12 program aims to reduce violence and support intercultural understanding. Resolving Conflict Creatively has been evaluated in four multiracial, multiethnic school districts in New York City and has demonstrated a positive change in classrooms, a decrease in physical violence in the classroom, and fewer episodes of verbal assault.

Children's Creative Response to Conflict (CCRC)

CCRC is considered one of the pioneers in conflict resolution education. The program is designed for children to learn actions of nonviolence at an early age. Cooperation, communication, affirmation, and conflict resolution are the original four themes of the program, which has been tested and proved over time in classrooms across America.

5

Peer Mediation Programming

"Maryanne and I just got into a big fight and she called me some pretty bad names. We used to be best friends, but ever since she started hanging out with Tonya, she's been really mean and doesn't do anything with me anymore. I'm really mad at Maryanne, but I wish I could still be her friend."—Lynn, age 13

"Lynn is just a big baby. We just got into this huge fight and she started calling me names. We used to be best friends, but she doesn't want to do anything together anymore. I'm hanging around with Tonya since she is new, and I can't believe how selfish Lynn is being by not being nice to her. I still want to be her friend, but I want to be friends with Tonya, too."—Maryanne, age 12

STUDENTS HELPING TO CREATE SAFE SCHOOLS

Maryanne and Lynn resolved their problem through one of the most widely used school safety programs in the United States—peer mediation. Lynn and Maryanne agreed to meet to try to resolve their conflict with the help of two trained mediators. Through the mediation process, Maryanne and Lynn communicated their feelings to each other and generated solutions themselves. The mediation resulted in a solution of having Tonya,

Maryanne, and Lynn taking time to play together and Lynn finding more quality "alone time" with Maryanne.

The spread of peer mediation programs around the country has outpaced research on its effects; as a result, there is much we still need to know about the effectiveness of peer mediation. Yet a wide variety of studies conducted in different locations and situations have found that peer mediation appears to be a promising strategy for improving the school climate.

Peer mediation programs help create safe schools by training students to serve as models for constructive conflict resolution and help peers mediate interpersonal conflicts. According to Bodine and Crawford (1998), peer mediation programs have been implemented for the following purposes:

- To provide an alternative to the consequences outlined in the school conduct code, such as suspensions and detentions
- To teach constructive problem solving
- As a classroom management technique
- To show students how to solve problems nonviolently and effectively and empower students who serve as peer mediators with the opportunity to help other students resolve their conflicts
- As a technique to improve the quality of the learning environment and safe schools

Peer mediation in elementary schools has been identified as a resource that promotes positive peer interactions and reduces school violence (S. Bell, Coleman, Anderson, Whelan, & Wilder, 2000; DeBaryshe & Fryxell, 1998; Powell, Muir-McClain, & Halasyamani, 1995). Fewer formal evaluations on peer mediation use in middle and high schools have been conducted, and those completed have resulted in contradictory outcomes. Theberge and Karan (2004) report that the most successful use of peer mediation was when students were exposed to the method in the early elementary grades and were reinforced for its use through high school. In addition, a combination of the two techniques (conflict resolution education and peer mediation) in the school is the most powerful method of helping students solve interpersonal problems in a constructive manner, which reduces the demonstration of violence and improving school safety (Maxwell, 1989).

GOALS AND PROCESS OF MEDIATION

Mediation is a process through which students and adults attempt to resolve their conflicts with the assistance of a third party who is trained in constructive conflict resolution techniques. As neutral third parties, mediators create an environment of support and confidentiality, which helps disputants discuss their problems and reach a mutually beneficial solution to the problem.

Mediation programs, which can be implemented in classrooms or school-wide, can help resolve student interpersonal conflict, student–teacher conflict, and conflicts between adults. Peer mediation can be offered to disputants for any number of reasons and regardless of whether the conflict occurs on or off school grounds. Mediations often involve conflicts over activities or behaviors that occur off-site over the weekend, during lunch, or on the bus to and from school. Issues concerning space or possessions are common among younger children, while issues of friendship, loyalty, and trust are most common topics for mediation among older students. The only topics student mediators should not mediate are conflicts concerning drug use, abuse, or some other form of criminal activity.

Mediation is not a recommended form of conflict resolution programming for students younger than seven years. Young students have cognitive limitations (particularly in perspective taking) and communication limitations that prohibit the successful use of the mediation process and the standard sequencing of steps in the process. School leaders are still encouraged to expose young students to the mediation process through adult model facilitation. In adult model facilitation, an adult helps young children tell their stories and generate solutions to a problem. Although it is unknown, empirically, how beneficial the adult model mediation is to young children, it appears to teach young students basic knowledge and skills helpful for future use of the mediation process—for example, to take turns while communicating and to generate multiple possible solutions for effective conflict resolution.

The role of trained mediators is to assist disputants in completing a six-step process, a process that remains the same regardless of its use with adults or students (Fisher, Ury, & Patton, 1991). As Figure 5.1 depicts, the six steps of mediation are (1) ensuring that disputants understand the mediation process, (2) identifying the conflict, (3) describing feelings and needs associated with the problem, (4) generating possible solutions, (5) discussing these options, and (6) selecting a solution.

Figure 5.1 The Six Steps of Mediation

These six steps are loosely based on the work of Fisher, Ury, and Patton (1991).

Step 1: Understanding the process

Step 2: Telling the story

Step 3: Describing feelings and identifying needs

Step 4: Generating solutions

Step 5: Evaluating options

Step 6: Agreeing to the solution

Step 1: Understanding the Process

Mediators first review with disputants the guidelines for the mediation process: (a) the purpose of mediation, (b) the role of the mediator as an unbiased third party, (c) the goal of resolving the conflict in a mutually satisfying manner, and (d) ground rules for behavior during the mediation (e.g., no name calling, swearing, aggression, etc.). Disputants must agree to the ground rules before the mediation process continues.

Step 2: Telling the Story

Once disputants understand and agree to the guidelines outlined in Step 1, each disputant has the opportunity to tell his or her side of the story uninterrupted. Mediators facilitate the process with active listening skills and by enforcing the ground rules of mediation. Mediators paraphrase the disputants' stories and ask for clarification if necessary.

Step 3: Describing Feelings and Identifying Needs

Once each disputant has had the opportunity to communicate his or her story, mediators help disputants describe their feelings about the conflict beyond those of anger and sadness. They encourage disputants to describe emotions such as frustration and hurt. In addition, mediators assist disputants in identifying needs associated with the conflict. Usually hidden by the outward source of conflict, needs must be uncovered during the mediation process. For instance, the conflict between Lynn and Maryanne in the chapter opening had little to do with the name calling but had a lot to do with the fear of losing a friend, a need embedded in belongingness and affiliation with others. Most conflicts resolve easily with mediation once needs are identified during the process.

Step 4: Generating Solutions

Next, disputants generate solutions based on the needs each outlined in Step 3. It is important that disputants, not mediators, create solutions to the problems. The success of mediation lies in mediators allowing conflict participants to resolve the conflict as opposed to telling disputants how to solve the conflict. Any solutions the disputants create are considered valid for the resolution, and mediators should not comment on or counsel the students about the proposed solutions. Solutions generated by disputants may not be equitable, but if the disputants agree to the solution, mediators cannot and should not intervene. However, mediators can ask open-ended questions such as "Can you think of any additional possible solutions?" and wait for disputants to create other solutions.

Step 5: Evaluating the Solutions

Mediators help disputants evaluate the outcomes they generated in Step 4 by discussing the solutions in context of the needs outlined in Step 3. For example, Lynn and Maryanne might have generated the following possible solutions: (1) Maryanne doesn't see Tonya anymore; (2) Lynn and Maryanne stop being friends; (3) Maryanne spends more time alone with Lynn; and (4) Lynn, Maryanne, and Tonya will play together sometimes. The role of the mediators is to have the disputants think about the viability of each of these possible solutions in relation to the problem. For instance, a mediator might say, "One suggestion to resolve this conflict is for Maryanne not to see Tonya anymore. Do you think this will resolve the conflict?" Lynn might say, "Great. Problem solved," but Maryanne will probably state that she won't accept this solution. The mediators proceed through each of the solutions until disputants select the most appropriate and mutually beneficial resolution.

Step 6: Agreeing to the Solution

Disputants decide on one solution for the conflict and commit to the solution. Often, they sign an agreement created by the mediators that outlines the resolution and "penalty" if disputants do not fulfill the agreement; for example, the penalty might be another round of mediation or a discussion with administration. The disputants and mediators sign the agreement to end the mediation. Mediators follow up with the disputants to assess the success of the mediation and the disputants' adherence to the agreement.

THEORETICAL FOUNDATION OF PEER MEDIATION

The purpose of peer mediation is to influence cognitive and social development, producing changes as disputants follow the model of mediators. Peer mediation has at its foundation traditional social learning and Vygotskian theory. Social learning theory posits that individuals mimic behaviors that they see (Bandura 1973; Patterson 1982), internalize these observed behaviors if they rehearse and view them as beneficial, and then spontaneously produce the behaviors during their disputes in the future. Hence, peer mediators serve as models of constructive conflict resolution strategies while assisting peers in the process of resolving conflicts. This process is similar to the learning process of the mediators. Stevahn, Johnson, Johnson, Laginski, and O'Coin (1996) found that high school students trained in peer mediation were more knowledgeable about constructive conflict resolution, retained the knowledge of the mediation process longer, and applied it to actual conflict situations as compared with students in a control group.

Social learning theorists, such as Albert Bandura, have investigated circumstances when students are most likely to initiate an imitation of a model. According to Bandura (1985), the factors that facilitate observational learning include (1) similarity of age of the model, (2) similarity of gender of the model, and (3) the person's learning history or experience in observational learning. So the success of mediation programming is, in part, due to the similarity of peer mediators to the disputants.

The significance of using peers in mediation is also grounded in the work of Vygotsky (1987). Cognitive development, according to Vygotsky, takes place as a result of social interactions, which guide children in the creation and use of new cognitive tools. Particularly important are social interactions with individuals who can guide, or scaffold, new information, or task knowledge, about a specific activity or behavior. Vygotsky emphasizes that cognitive changes occur when the individual's problem solving is guided by another person within the individual's "zone of proximal development," or area of cognitive expertise. Since peers are more likely to exist within similar zones of proximal development as compared with adults, trained peers are more likely to guide cognitive changes related to peer mediation principles and processes and constructive methods of conflict resolution. Although not empirically supported, the theories of Vygotsky and Bandura suggest that the use of peers as models of mediation heightens the potential internalization of the process by disputants, which increases the likelihood of cognitive changes.

SCHOOL STAFF INVOLVEMENT IN PEER MEDIATION PROGRAMS

Although individual classrooms can use peer mediation, it is more common that a school or district implements a peer mediation program. Peer mediation program development and implementation requires a commitment from all adults in the school community. Administrators, staff, and faculty must model mediation skills in their interactions with students, families, and with each other and encourage students to do the same. All staff members, including paraprofessionals, bus drivers, and lunchroom aides, require ongoing training on the mediation process. Therefore, before school leaders implement a peer mediation program, they must establish a program development and implementation timeline that includes staff orientation and professional development (see Figure 5.2).

A staff informational meeting and staff development opportunities should be separate events when developing and implementing a peer mediation program. Staff should receive an orientation concerning the peer mediation program, how it will work, how staff will be involved, when it will occur, and how they can volunteer to assist with the program. This meeting should also include a brief overview of research in the field on peer

Figure 5.2   Peer Mediation Program Development and Implementation
Sample

School safety teams can use the following event line with its progression of goals as a
guide to establishing a timeline for mediation program implementation.

Step 1: Preliminary Program Development

- Establish an advisory committee to oversee the administration of the program and
  help troubleshoot and publicize the program. (Since many schools do not have the
  personnel for an advisory committee, the school may wish to use a subcommittee
  from the school safety team.)
- Designate program coordinators who schedule mediations, select appropriate
  conflicts to mediate, and assign mediators.
- Develop a peer mediation program plan. The plan might include a timetable for
  implementation and review of the program and the process of evaluation of the
  program. (The school may wish to use the school safety team plan as the basis.)
- Create procedures and administrative guidelines for such areas as the number of
  mediations per day, when they will occur, where, how to recruit mediators, and so on.
- Present plan to staff at informational meeting.

Step 2: Program Implementation

- Train mediation trainers.
- Provide professional development workshop to staff.
- Promote program throughout school.
- Present program to students through school assembly and/or classroom presentations.
- Select peer mediators.
- Assess pretraining variables of skills, knowledge, and attitudes.
- Train peer mediators.
- Provide continuous follow-up support for mediators.

Step 3: Program Evaluation

- Assess posttraining variables of skills, knowledge, and attitudes.
- Collect measures of changes in discipline and conduct of students, including
  incident reports, suspensions, and numbers of mediations.
- Review training program for continued use.
- Begin identification of new mediators.

mediation and school safety and a refresher on the benefits of social skills
training in schools. Creating the connection between academic competency,
student resilience, and social skills training is important. Hawkins (1992)
and Bernard (1993) are good sources to provide staff during this discussion.
Staff should also be informed if the process is available for use in adult and
student–adult conflicts.

A staff development meeting should occur shortly before the training of
peer mediators. It is critical that staff receives training or a brief refresher on
the merits of conflict and effective methods of resolving conflict and has
opportunities to practice the mediation process with commonly occurring

conflicts. To serve as advocates of the program, staff members need to be involved in the program and understand the process students will use during peer mediation. A staff development session is one of the best methods for increasing support for the program and establishing its stability within the schools. Once staff members are familiar with the program and its benefits, they often volunteer to serve as trainers for the peer mediators or volunteers for preparing materials for the peer mediation room. One of the surest ways to decrease the likelihood of program success is to leave school staff out of the program. Although staff might not be involved directly with program implementation, the relationship between teacher knowledge and support and program effectiveness is quite high.

IMPLEMENTING PEER MEDIATION PROGRAMS

Program guides are available to assist school leaders with peer mediation implementation. See publications such as *Peer Mediation: Conflict Resolution in the School Program Guide* by Schrumpf, Crawford, and Usafel (1991) and *Student Mediation in Elementary Schools* by the National Resource Center for Youth Mediation (1995).

The following discussion provides strategies for implementing peer mediation programs in schools.

Selecting Students for Peer Mediation Training

Schools may use several techniques to select students to participate in peer mediation programs, including teacher selection, student nomination, or a combination of both teacher and student recommendation. The preferable method of selecting peer mediators is through a nomination ballot. (Examples of nomination forms appear in Figures 5.3 and 5.4, and a permission letter for parents/guardians to sign appears in Figure 5.5.) Students can nominate themselves or other students to become peer mediators. Final selection of mediators occurs with teacher input.

Students selected as peer mediators should represent a cross section of the school's student population. The group's demographics should mirror those of the student population with adequate representation of ethnicity and race. In school communities with little ethnic or racial diversity, it is still important to include students from all established peer groups in the school. As mentioned previously, the similarity of mediators to the disputants influences peer mediation program effectiveness; therefore, mediators should be available to handle conflicts of students in similar peer groups.

Students should not be selected to participate in peer mediation programs based on academic abilities or behavior demonstrated in the classroom. In fact, sometimes, the best mediators are students who have a long history as disputants of conflict.

Figure 5.3   Sample Nomination Ballot for Peer Mediators

Self-Nomination

We need your help in finding the best peer mediators for our new school peer mediation program. Do you or does someone you know fit the following criteria?

Do you have	Leadership Ability?
	Good Verbal Skills?
Do you show	Respect and Trustworthiness?
Do you agree	to Commit to the Peer Mediation Program?

If you answered yes to all of these questions or know someone in the school who might answer yes, please complete the bottom of the form.

❑ I want to become a peer mediator. My name is _____, my grade is _____, and my homeroom teacher is _____.

❑ I want to nominate someone to be a peer mediator. His/Her name is _____, his/her grade is _____, and his/her homeroom teacher is _____.

Figure 5.4   Sample Peer Mediation Application Form

Name:_____

Grade: _____

Age: _____ Male/Female _____

Directions: Please answer the following questions and return the completed application form to Ms. Casey in the peer mediation room.

1. I want to become a peer mediator because

2. I think I would make an effective peer mediator because

3. I think peer mediation is a good idea for our school because

4. I would use peer mediation to help resolve conflicts such as

If I am selected as a peer mediator, I understand that I must attend the training session and the follow-up meetings. I also agree that I will keep up with my schoolwork and make up any classroom work I miss.

_____   _____
Student Signature   Date

(Continued)

Figure 5.4 (Continued)

Teacher Recommendation

    ❑ Yes, I recommend this student.

    ❑ No, I do not recommend this student at this time.

Strengths: Areas to improve:

_____   _____

Teacher Signature   Date

Figure 5.5   Sample Parent Permission Letter

Dear Parent/Guardian:

We are pleased to offer your son/daughter _____the opportunity to participate in the Peer Mediation program at school. The program trains selected students as mediators who help other students find positive ways to solve disagreements. We believe the mediation program will provide all members of the school community with invaluable life skills that will promote safe school practices.

Your son/daughter has been identified by his/her classmates and teacher as a leader in the school and as a good choice for the program. As a mediator in the Peer Mediation program, your child will participate in a three-day training session, will be required to attend meetings twice each month, and will need to make up any class work missed as a result of participation in the program.

If your child has permission to participate in the Peer Mediation program, please sign the form below and ask your child to return it to his or her homeroom teacher tomorrow.

If you have any questions regarding the program and your son's/daughter's involvement as a peer mediator, please feel free to contact me at (777) 555-1234.

Sincerely,

Principal _____

-------------------✂------------------------------✂--------------------

PERMISSION FORM

_____ has my permission to participate in the Peer Mediation program as a trained peer mediator.

_____   _____

Signature (Parent or Guardian)   Date

Peer mediators should be selected based on the following criteria:

- Commitment to the concept of peaceful conflict resolution
- Willingness to participate in the program
- Leadership qualities
- Permission to participate from parents
- Understanding of confidentiality surrounding the procedure

The number of students selected to participate in peer mediation programs varies according to the type of program desired. Schoolwide approaches require a larger number of peer mediators to be trained than programs confined to a classroom; an ideal ratio would be 2 mediators for every 40 students. Also, training of peer mediators should not take place with groups larger than 30 per 3 facilitators. Larger schools should stagger training sessions to accommodate larger numbers of students.

School leaders can introduce the program to the student body through a school assembly, role-playing to demonstrate the principles and concepts of peer mediation. Some schools use local theater or puppet groups at these assemblies to introduce students to the program.

Selecting Mediation Program Coordinators

Successful peer mediation programs often take a great deal of time, as least initially. The persons responsible for the program should meet the following criteria:

- Belief that school safety programs benefit students cognitively and socially
- An ability to organize materials required for the program on an ongoing basis
- A willingness to train other adults in peer mediation programming
- Time available for programming needs, depending on the size of the program and support available. Count on at least 15 to 20 hours per week to handle a small-scale program.

Some schools hire peer mediation coordinators to implement and maintain the program. School leaders should appoint more than one coordinator, if possible, as programs can be deeply affected by the departure of a coordinator. Individuals responsible for the peer mediation program must also be able to train students in the peer mediation process. It is a worthwhile investment to pay for an outside consultant to train mediation coordinators and several other volunteers, such as noon aides, parent volunteers, and a school counselor, in a train-the-trainer program before the student training. Train-the-trainer programs involve two components: student-training techniques and peer mediation program content. Therefore, coordinators are familiar with the mediation process, administering and maintaining the program, and training students in the material. (The recommended training time is a minimum of 20 hours.) School leaders should also consider using the experienced consultant to assist mediation coordinators with the student training for the first program year.

Training Peer Mediators

Peer mediation training takes at least three full days because of the necessary administrative information that must be provided in addition to the training of critical learning points. Three days also gives students time to develop a thorough understanding of the process, time to become more committed to the program, and time for greater exploration of peaceful conflict resolution. Often, students need to miss scheduled classes to attend training sessions. Training times may occur during school, after school, during evenings, on weekends, or any combination of the above. It is very important, however, to schedule the training sessions as close together as possible to reinforce critical material. In addition, peer mediators need to create group cohesion as quickly as possible, and closely scheduled training is the best way to accomplish this. Varying the time of day for each training session minimizes the total time students miss any one particular class but can interfere with building group cohesion and the learning process.

In many cases, peer mediation training is a scheduled course, where students receive credit for its completion and students need not be pulled from other courses. A list of resources available for training students in mediation and negotiation and administering and developing programs appears in Appendix C. A sample peer mediation training agenda for students appears in Figure 5.6.

Training peer mediators involves four essential components:

1. Program logistics, including when mediations will occur, where mediations will occur, how mediators will be paired, and other similar issues

2. Discussion of conflict and its essential usefulness to human development

3. Skills associated with effective peer mediation, including effective communication and perspective-taking skills

4. The role of the mediator and the mediation process

Marzano (1992) outlines a method for teaching students procedural knowledge—that is, providing learners with a general set of rules for how to do something (mediating conflicts) as opposed to imparting information. Marzano's three-part model for teaching the peer mediation process consists of (1) constructing models, (2) shaping, and (3) internalizing.

Figure 5.6   Sample Training Agenda—Three Days

Peer Mediators—Core Training for Secondary Students

Day 1	
8:30–9:00	Icebreaker
9:00–9:15	Welcome and overview of the training
9:15–9:45	Introduction to mediation and the peer mediation program
9:45–10:30	Conflict and opportunity
10:30–10:45	Break
10:45–11:30	What is a peer mediator?
11:30–12:00	What makes an effective peer mediator?
12:00–12:45	Lunch
12:45–1:30	Communication skills (*I* messages and active listening skills)
1:30–2:00	Perspective taking
2:00–2:15	Break
2:15–3:00	Mediation process
3:00–3:15	Wrap-up and review
Day 2	
8:30–9:00	Icebreaker
9:00–9:15	Mediation process review
9:15–9:25	Beginning the process
9:25–9:45	Gathering information
9:45–10:30	Identifying needs
10:30–10:45	Break
10:45–12:00	Generating solutions
12:00–12:45	Lunch
12:45–1:30	Evaluating solutions
1:30–2:00	Writing an agreement
2:00–2:15	Break
2:15–3:00	Review and role-play exercise
3:00–3:15	Wrap-up

(Continued)

Figure 5.6 (Continued)

Day 3	
8:30–9:00	Icebreaker
9:00–10:30	Role-play exercises
10:30–10:45	Break
10:45–12:00	Potential pitfalls
12:00–12:45	Lunch
12:45–1:15	The mediation room
1:15–2:00	Referral and scheduling process
2:00–2:15	Break
2:15–2:45	Confidentiality
2:45–3:15	Wrap-up and ceremony

Marzano states that procedural learning must be constructive in nature. Individuals learn procedures for behaving and thinking, and during real-life situations, they adapt the procedures to the mental map of those learned during training. Once the learners (peer mediators) have constructed a mental model of the mediation process, the next step is training them to shape and modify the six-step mediation process as they learn it. According to Marzano, shaping is critical to developing procedural knowledge because it assists in generalizing processes to other situations and truly understanding procedural processes. Procedural learning is complete when internalization of information has occurred. Mediation becomes an automatic process after internalization.

In procedural learning, trainers must employ a variety of techniques so that students can construct appropriate models for mediation, shape behavior to meet the needs of the mediation situation, and internalize the process. Trainers should provide plenty of opportunities for students to rehearse skills learned during training and provide follow-up over a number of months. (Peer mediators should meet together at least twice a month or every other week to discuss both successful and difficult mediation, with the coordinators serving as leaders.) Exercises should be interactive and repetitive and include role-playing as a central strategy. Role-play exercises are highly important for peer mediation training because they assist student mediators with rehearsing the six-step mediation process and practicing working with disputants. They also can provide student mediators with experience with scenarios of difficult mediations and how to troubleshoot during the process. Unlike a recipe, where one can throw ingredients in all at once or out of order, the six-step mediation process is concrete and inflexible. Mediators must learn how to return to the process if the disputants deviate from it. For instance, peer mediators must know that disputants evaluate possible solutions after they generate them and that an agreement follows this step. If disputants return to a discussion of their feelings on the conflict while evaluating solutions, the mediators must be mindful of which step in the process is on the table and must think of a way to maneuver the disputants back to evaluating the solutions.

The coordinator can create the role-play situations, but more often, the basis of the mediators' meetings involves role-playing real cases. Videotaping student mediators helps students create mental maps, adapt their mediation techniques, and build their skills by watching others. Role-play exercises are best in controlled settings with clear goals and objectives—for example, for the first six role-plays, mediators practice the six-step process, and the next six, they practice what to do when the disputants don't generate solutions. Sample guidelines for role-play exercises appear in Figure 5.7.

Figure 5.7   Role-Play Guidelines for Mediation Coordinators

- Instruct peer mediators how to give appropriate feedback concerning a disputant's behavior, not the disputant. Student mediators should use the 2 + 2 method of reinforcement: say two nice things about the person's behavior and counter them with two suggestions for improvement.
- Reinforce mediators who give appropriate feedback.
- Demonstrate feedback skills during the exercise, using specific examples and statements.
- Ask open-ended questions that promote discussion, such as the examples that follow.

Ask the Actors:

- How did you feel playing the role?
- What did you notice yourself doing? (Encourage students to respond to their actions and words. The more general purpose of the exercise is one of introspection initially. Once students become more experienced with role-playing, they can begin to critique their words and communication strategies.)
- How did the other person(s) respond to your actions and words?

Ask the Observers:

- How did you feel as you watched your peers participate in the role-play exercise? (The purpose of this question is to begin a discussion. Students might provide responses such as *frustrated*—they may have wanted to jump in and help the mediators at a critical point; *angry*—at the disputants who wouldn't stick to the agreed-upon rules; *pleased*—the disputants reached an agreement.)
- What stands out about the disputants' behavior?
- What might the students playing the mediators do differently?

(Continued)

Figure 5.7 (Continued)

ROLE-PLAY SUGGESTIONS

Situation 1

Student 1: You are best friends with Student 2. A new student comes to the school, and Student 2 now spends more time with him or her and less time with you.

Student 2: You are best friends with Student 1. A new student comes to the school, and you feel sorry that he or she doesn't have any friends. You don't think your friendship with the new student should hurt your friendship with Student 1.

Situation 2

Student 1: You are standing by your locker and are suddenly bumped from behind. You are hit so hard that you drop your books on the floor.

Student 2: You are walking down the hall and a door suddenly opens, forcing you to walk right into another student at his or her locker. You didn't mean to bump him or her.

Situation 3

Student 1: You have just broken up with a significant other. You find out that a friend is now dating your ex. It was a really difficult breakup, and you are hurt that your friend moved in so quickly.

Student 2: You have gotten close to Student 1's ex over the last few months. When your friend ended the relationship, you thought it was okay to start dating your friend's ex.

Situation 4

Student 1: You are close friends with Student 2. Student 2 asks to borrow your favorite video game. Student 2 returns the video game weeks later, and it is broken.

Student 2: You are best friends with Student 1. You ask to borrow a video game Student 1 rarely plays. You return it a couple of weeks later. You didn't realize that it was Student 1's favorite game, and besides, you couldn't even play the game because it was broken.

CONDUCTING THE PEER MEDIATION PROGRAM

Procedures for running peer mediation programs depend largely on individual school factors, such as space and time constraints and when peer mediation can be most effective. Peer mediation is not always effective, for example, when conducted right after school, when students are eager to leave and will agree to anything just so they can go home. When establishing basic procedures for peer mediation programming, program coordinators must consider how the mediation referral process will occur, when students will mediate, and what conflicts students will mediate.

Mediation Referrals and Requests

Students who wish to participate in mediation complete peer mediation request forms. Students, teachers, parents, and administrative and support staff who feel that mediation should occur may also complete these forms. Request forms should be available throughout the school, including outside the main office and in classrooms, the school library, the cafeteria, and the mediation center itself. A sample mediation request form for middle and high school appears in Figure 5.8. The request for mediation has to be anonymous for students to feel comfortable with the process. Completed request forms are placed in locked boxes, also located throughout the school, to encourage whole school participation and retain the confidentiality of the process.

Schools that implement a peer mediation program often don't get a lot of business in the program's first few months, because students do not feel comfortable with the thought of having someone help them resolve their conflicts. Instead, the peer mediation program serves as the alternative process for students at risk for suspensions and detentions. To build on these cases, program coordinators and peer mediators must publicize the availability of the program to the student body. Mediators might perform skits in classrooms to demonstrate the process, or coordinators might videotape a scenario resolved through peer mediation and show the tape in each classroom. Students will use the program when they feel comfortable knowing more about what will happen in the room and are less concerned with confidentiality issues.

Figure 5.8   Sample Peer Mediation Request Form Sample

Date: _____

Names and grade levels of students involved in disagreement: _____

Where did the disagreement occur?	What was the disagreement about?
_____ Classroom	_____ Personal property
_____ Hallway	_____ Name calling
_____ Cafeteria	_____ Friendship
_____ Outside	_____ Fighting
_____ Other	_____ Other

When did the disagreement occur? _____

Briefly describe the disagreement: _____

Person requesting mediation: _____ Student _____ Teacher _____ Counselor _____ Administrator _____ Other

Name of person requesting mediation (optional): _____

Mediation program coordinators are responsible for logging in all requests for mediations and scheduling mediations. It is critical that coordinators carefully screen the mediation requests for a number of factors, such as the following:

• *Can mediation resolve the conflict?* Students should not mediate conflicts involving alcohol and drug use, sexual abuse, or other criminal behavior. Coordinators should acknowledge the mediation request and facilitate assistance with the conflict by contacting school counselors/social workers. Disputes handled by peer mediators often include issues of property, gossip/ rumors, friendship, and name-calling. Controversy surrounds the use of mediation for conflicts resulting from bully–victim relationships. If coordinators become aware of a conflict referred to mediation that has, as its root, bullying, consider an adult-facilitated mediation. The presence of peer mediators may incite bullying behaviors and increase the anxiety felt by a victim confronted by a bully during the mediation.

• *Are the disputants willing to receive mediation?* Coordinators find some time during the school day to ask the disputants if they wish to go through the mediation process. Coordinators describe the program, explain the mediation procedure, and determine disputants' interest before scheduling mediation. Peer mediation is always voluntary and should not be scheduled if one (or both) of the disputants is unwilling to participate. Mediation coordinators circumvent a great number of problems by ensuring individual interest in the process.

Once coordinators have determined interest in peer mediation by both disputants, the coordinator schedules the time and location (if other than the mediation center) the mediation is to occur. Coordinators should match peer mediators to conflict situations based on the nature of the conflict, the complexity of the conflict, and the gender/racial/ethnic background of the disputants. Coordinators should ask mediators if their friendship with a disputant might interfere with their objectivity during the mediation. To reduce the likelihood of bias, coordinators should not schedule mediators who are friends with disputants.

All mediations should have comediators; two student mediators are preferable. The mediation process is more difficult with more than two mediators, as only one mediator should talk at once. But a mediator benefits by having a backup in case he or she misses a mediation step or disputants need to caucus before completing the process. Sometimes, with a seemingly difficult mediation, the adult coordinator may wish to sit in with the two peer mediators. Coordinators should use many mediation opportunities to place highly skilled mediators with those needing additional assistance. Working with a skilled mediator provides excellent training opportunities for new mediators or students who are uncomfortable leading the mediation process. Coordinators should not schedule peer mediations with more than two disputants. If more than two students involved in a conflict wish to take part in the mediation process, an adult should comediate with the two peer mediators.

Mediation Location and Time

The first choices for peer mediation times should be before school or during lunchtime, homeroom, study hall, or library time. Mediations may take as little as ten minutes or as long as a few days to complete. Coordinators should not allow student mediations to take more than two class periods in one day, with no more than two days spent on mediation. The location of peer mediations depends on the school's resources. A dedicated peer mediation room is preferable for both elementary and secondary school children, with this room available for mediations at least one or more class periods each day at regular hours of operation. The mediation room should be separate from the traditional disciplinary offices, such as the main office, but close to one of the mediation coordinators' classrooms. Ideally, the mediation room has an anteroom or large separator so an adult can be close enough to assist in mediation if absolutely necessary but the integrity of a confidential setting is maintained.

If schools cannot dedicate a space the first year of programming, mediators can use hallways for mediation as long as they afford privacy to the disputants and the mediators while maintaining security and close proximity to adult supervision. Elementary school children can easily mediate conflict on the playground, in the hallway, or even in the cafeteria if privacy is secured. For instance, many schools schedule peer mediators on the playground where much conflict occurs (particularly during lunch). Mediators stand "post" at a variety of locations on the playground and handle conflicts referred by disputants themselves or by lunch aides. Mediation coordinators schedule mediators on the playground but rarely more than one time per week.

The mediation center works best, however, for secondary grades, as it provides the greatest opportunity for confidentiality. Peer mediators should also be allowed to consider this as their working room. School leaders should consider purchasing conflict resolution and stress and anger management materials for students, as well as large, colorful posters depicting similar concepts for the walls.

Potential Problems and Solutions
Encountered in Peer Mediation Programming

Several problems might inhibit the success of peer mediation programming. These include the following.

Students' Attitudes Regarding Mediation

Many students are uncomfortable with the process of mediation and, therefore, will never voluntarily agree to participate. Students have been known to distrust mediation due to confidentiality concerns and prefer to resolve their conflicts autonomously. On the other hand, some students may exclusively use mediation as a technique to resolve conflict.

- *What to do if confidentiality is violated.* One of the important principles of peer mediation is confidentiality among disputants and mediators. There really isn't a way to retain confidentiality among disputants, who often freely discuss the outcome of the mediation, but their discussion of the process to others might actually promote the use of the program by other students. Mediation coordinators must, however, address a violation of confidentiality by mediators immediately. If violations of confidentiality continue, the individual need not leave the program, but coordinators should use the person less frequently for sensitive mediations. Peer mediators should be encouraged to discuss mediations during follow-up meetings with other mediators and program coordinators. These discussions with other peer mediators, particularly about difficult or unresolved mediations, should not include the names of disputants. Disclosure of disputants' names in conversations should occur only between mediators and mediation coordinators.
- *What to do if a student constantly seeks peer mediation as a conflict resolution technique.* A student who consistently seeks peer mediation to resolve conflicts might be reinforced by its many positive benefits. More likely, however, the student enjoys the personal attention mediators give to his or her problems or is eager to get out of class. In this situation, coordinators should limit mediations to one per week and refer the individual to the school counselor. Coordinators might consider training the disputant as a mediator, as he or she will be extremely experienced in the process!

Mediation Process Concerns

The process may be ineffective because of challenges the mediators experience, often due to training deficiencies. Student mediators must be carefully screened and trained for the maximum benefit.

- *What to do if disputants do not reach an agreement.* Some mediations may not end with an agreement. Mediators should learn when to end the process and suggest alternatives to resolving the conflict, such as continuing the mediation on another day, caucusing separately with the disputants, continuing the mediation with different mediators, or meeting with a school counselor. When mediators caucus with the disputants, they separate the disputants, and one mediator talks with one disputant while the other disputant remains with the other mediator. During a caucus, the mediator establishes if the disputant wishes or is able to continue with the mediation (sometimes the disputant is crying or very upset) and whether the disputant is willing to reach a solution to the conflict.

- *What to do if an agreement is broken.* If an agreement is broken, usually one of the disputants will request another mediation. Conducting a second mediation and bringing it to a resolution works in most cases. If an agreement is broken a second time, mediators should refer the individuals to a school counselor or administrator.
- *What to do if a mediator gets in trouble.* Coordinators should clearly state that peer mediators will always remain peer mediators regardless of academic performance or classroom behavioral problems. It is very important that students understand that they are learning life skills, and that life skills can never be taken away. Also, participation in peer mediation should never be part of disciplinary action. One of the coordinators should discuss the trouble with the mediator and attempt to resolve the problem. If the behavior continues, coordinators should use the mediator less frequently.

CREATING FAMILY AND COMMUNITY PARTNERSHIPS

Family and community partnerships can be extremely useful when implementing peer mediation programs in the schools. Indeed, to increase the effectiveness of peer mediation, students who are exposed to the mediation process in school should also be able to use the process consistently at home and in the community. Gentry and Benenson (1993) note that informed parents of peer mediators reported a significant decline in the frequency and intensity of students' conflicts with siblings and in conflicts perceived to need parental intervention.

Certainly, the school safety team should assist in peer mediation program implementation and creating partnerships within the community. Team members should consider participating in the train-the-trainer program so they can assist with training student mediators and providing informational workshops for parents on the administration of the program and the content of the training. Team members who are parents may also want to receive specialized training to provide seminars on family communication and problem-solving skills with suggestions for using mediation in the home.

Interested team members might wish to continue their learning experiences and volunteer in community mediation centers. The American Bar Association supports community mediation sites in all 50 states, where volunteers mediate disputes within the community. These community mediation volunteers might also educate school faculty on understanding the types of disputes referred to community mediation programs, as some disputes benefit from cross-referrals between school-based and community-based mediation sessions. For instance, student conflict in the classroom may be the result of neighborhood friction between the parents of the two students. In such cases, the school-based and community-based mediation team together might be more effective in resolving this conflict than a school-based or community-based center alone. Student peer mediators might also benefit from internship opportunities provided by community mediation centers.

APPLICATION OF
THE MEDIATION MODEL

Case Study

Samuel is a fourth-grade student in a large urban school district. He has been absent 56 days since the beginning of the school year, with only two months left. Samuel has medical issues, including sudden and violent epileptic seizures that last for quite some time. Samuel is forced to wear protective headgear. The headgear is ill fitting and unattractive, which encourages other students to bully Samuel consistently. Frustrated with the other students and his situation, Samuel threatened other students with violence. He was suspended for three days and is currently on probation. Samuel has the aptitude to perform, but his poor attendance is having a tremendous impact.

Truancy mediation helped Samuel and diffused the potentially violent situation at the school. Samuel, his mother, and school administrators engaged in the mediation process to problem-solve the difficult situation. The trained adult mediator guided the process so that Samuel was able to verbalize his frustration with the outdated headgear and the bullying from other children. Samuel's mother was able to identify how her limited resources prevented her from buying Samuel appropriate and attractive headgear. Through mediation, participants brainstormed ways to support the purchase of new headgear and strategies for confronting bullying behaviors, and they alleviated student and parent concerns about attendance.

School safety and truancy are closely linked. Truancy has been clearly identified as one of the early warning signs that youth potentially are headed for delinquent activity, social isolation, or educational failure. Several studies have established lack of commitment to school as a risk factor for substance abuse, delinquency, teen pregnancy, and dropping out of school (A. Bell, Rosen, & Dynlacht, 1994; Dryfoos, 1990; Huizinga, Loeber, & Thornberry, 1995; Rohrman, 1993). In addition, decades of research have identified a link between truancy and later problems, such as violence, marital problems, job problems, adult criminality, and incarceration (Catalano, Arthur, Hawkins, Berglund, & Olson, 1998; Dryfoos, 1990; Robins & Ratcliff, 1978; Snyder & Sickmund, 1995). Significant numbers of truant students also may signal a school environment that is unsafe for victimized students.

Truancy mediation is being found useful for addressing the underlying causes of truant students in K–12 school. Due to the structure of the court system and the limited amount of time judges and referees have to spend on each case, parties in mediation can arrive at agreements and results that a court may not be able to achieve. Because parties in a mediation can often find the most effective solution for their own problem, there is a greater chance that the problem will be resolved.

Created in 1999, the Truancy Prevention Through Mediation Program (TPTM) was developed to reduce school absenteeism by holding truancy mediation sessions with a teacher, a parent or guardian of the targeted child, and a neutral third-party mediator. TPTM uses a facilitated problem-solving session mediated by an uninvolved and well-trained third party, the mediator, to address student truancy. The goal is to, in a nonpunitive, nondisciplinary way, identify the family problems that, often, are causing the poor attendance and then to help the family reach a voluntary solution. Those solutions often involve reaching out to a government agency, social service provider, or nonprofit organization. Truancy mediation programs create an atmosphere where there is a free flow of information and a better understanding of the child's views and interests than a court might ever hear.

Mediations usually take place in the school during or immediately before or after school hours. In Grades K–6, the teacher attends and often is the only person meeting with the parent/guardian. This is because the teacher is viewed as a coparent, and the parent/guardian and the teacher meet to share their mutual concern for the student. In many cases, this is the first time the teacher and parent/guardian have met.

An adaptation of the model, developed and used by the Ohio Commission on Dispute Resolution and Conflict Management (1999), is being piloted through the Wayne County (Michigan) Prosecutor's Office. Attorneys in Wayne County have developed a working relationship with schools, social service agencies, and community organizations to offer solutions to the problems of truancy. Since the program began, 26 school districts in the metropolitan Detroit area have adopted the program.

MODELS OF EFFECTIVE PEER MEDIATION PROGRAMMING

Conflict Managers Program

San Francisco Community Board has been successfully implementing peer mediation programs in the San Francisco area since 1982. Conflict managers trained by school personnel often mediate conflicts on the playground. The organization's self-evaluation of effectiveness indicates a decrease in conflict in San Francisco schools (Community Boards, 2008).

Peers Making Peace (PMP)

PMP is an innovative peer mediation program that uses a preventive approach for handling conflicts both in and out of school. The program is based on a combination of strategies that include life and social skills training, conflict prevention and resolution, and peer-led modeling and coaching. The goal of the program is to improve school environments by reducing violence, assaults, and discipline referrals and by increasing academic performance. This is accomplished by training teams of students.

Teaching Students to Be Peacemakers Program (TSPP)

Developed by David and Roger Johnson, TSPP is a 12-year conflict resolution program in which students learn increasingly sophisticated negotiation and mediation procedures each year. It concentrates on teaching students how to value constructive conflict, engage in problem solving and integrative negotiations, and mediate classmates' conflicts. The intent is to provide each student with at least 12 years of training in how to manage conflicts constructively and thereby significantly change the way they manage their conflicts for the rest of their lives.

Johnson and Johnson (2001) conducted a meta-analysis of 17 evaluation studies examining TSPP effectiveness in eight schools in two countries. Results indicated that students learned the conflict resolution procedures taught, retained their knowledge throughout the school year, applied the knowledge to actual conflicts, transferred skills to nonclassroom and nonschool settings, and used the skills similarly in family and school settings.

6

Integrating Diversity Into Conflict Resolution Education Programs

Greenfield High School is located in a wealthy, predominantly White, suburb of a large urban area. Over the past year, Greenfield has experienced some considerable changes. Academically, the school has failed to meet its annual yearly progress (AYP) measures for the first time in its long history. The school has had to hire three additional special education learning specialists to address student challenges. Student conflicts have heightened. Fights inside the school, on campus grounds, and at school-sanctioned functions off-site have increased exponentially. Racially based hate symbols have appeared on the walls of the bathroom. Parents and guardians are demonstrating considerable concern by storming the district school board meetings. Students are leaving the district for private and independent schools in the neighborhood.

In the past year, Greenfield has gone from a 98 percent White, upper-middle- to lower-upper-class population to a 67 percent White population with varying socioeconomic backgrounds. The national housing market has transformed the community from having a 95 percent owner-occupied rate to a 83 percent rate. Many renters of the now affordable homes are racially and ethnically different from the long-term homeowners.

Staff and administrators are unsure as to how to stop the flow of students out of the district, ensure academic excellence for all youth, and address the conduct issues that are becoming disruptive to classroom management and the school's functioning.

SAFE SCHOOLS APPRECIATE DIFFERENCES

Greenfield School highlights a significant trend in schools across America. As this nation's schools' demographics change, as a result of immigration, urban sprawl, and economic conditions among other reasons, school administrators are faced with addressing challenges that arise from an increasing diverse student population. As the diversity of the student population increases, so do the culturally based conflicts that are exacerbated by differences in language, culture, ideological beliefs, and other characteristics between marginalized youth and the mainstream student population. The consequences of these values and behavioral differences are often strained interpersonal relationships among and between groups with differences (Brinson, Lovett, & Price, 2004). Unprepared K–12 administrators and teachers, as those depicted in the case study, place student achievement and school safety at risk.

Safe schools are schools in which all youth, regardless of race, religion, gender, sexual orientation, socioeconomic status, ability, or ethnicity, feel safe and accepted in the classroom and the hallways in schools they attend. In the 2005 School Crime Supplement to the National Crime Victimization Survey, students ages 12–18 were asked if someone at school had called them a derogatory word having to do with their race, ethnicity, religion, disability, gender, or sexual orientation and if they had seen hate-related graffiti during the previous six months. Some 11 percent of the students surveyed reported that someone at school had used hate-related words against them, and more than one-third (38 percent) had seen hate-related graffiti at school (NCES & BJS, 2005).

Diversity and inclusion education is now a necessary component of building safer schools amidst the growing pluralism of American classrooms. Once limited to the instruction of customs and languages of different ethnic groups around the world, diversity and inclusion education in schools today facilitates a school environment that is conducive to student learning. To meet this challenge, teachers must employ not only theoretically sound but also culturally responsive pedagogy.

> Culturally responsive pedagogy facilitates and supports the achievement of all students. In a culturally responsive classroom, effective teaching and learning occur in a culturally supported, learner-centered context, whereby the strengths students bring to school are identified, nurtured, and utilized to promote student achievement.

Diversity education has a strong connection to conflict resolution education in the schools. At its most basic level, conflict is the result of opposition between two or more individuals. Because diversity is the essence of differences among people, disagreements about opinions and behaviors will occur among diverse populations. Conflict that occurs among students about thoughts and behaviors are often compounded and more emotionally charged by ethnicity, race, religion, age, gender, ability, and socioeconomic status differences. For instance, two children fight over a swing on the playground. Differences in the students' race increase their hostility. In addition to physical fighting over the swing, the students shout racial slurs at one another, heightening the destructive nature of the conflict. In this case, conflict resolution must address the source of the conflict (swing turn taking), as well as the source of bias demonstrated during the conflict situation. Conflicts that result from differences in ethnicity, race, religion, age, gender, ability, and socioeconomic status often cannot all be resolved through traditional conflict resolution techniques but rather must be addressed through the lens of diversity. Cross-cultural problem solving requires a recognition of and respect for individual differences between and the commonalities across human experience.

When used together, conflict resolution education and diversity education can be incredibly powerful. They can challenge deeply ingrained belief systems and teach tolerance, acceptance, and respect through effective communicating, sophisticated perspective taking, and constructive conflict resolution strategies.

GOALS OF DIVERSITY EDUCATION

The primary goal of diversity education is to improve intercultural relations among students. Since the early 1990s, two popular approaches to improving tolerance and sensitivity to individual differences through diversity education have emerged: school reform and student learning.

School Reform

School reform approaches to combat prejudice involve systemic changes in the school related to student biases and prejudice. Systemic changes, according to Banks (1994), involve developing multicultural content throughout the curriculum and providing opportunities to learn and incorporate a variety of different viewpoints into the curriculum. While school reform is a worthwhile concept, it is uncertain whether changes will occur in the schools without public policy mandates and funding appropriations supporting these initiatives. Increasingly, researchers have identified that school reform efforts have been limited to issues of race and not the broader definition of diversity and that only certain areas have been identified for reform. For instance, many states have implemented antibullying policies, protecting students from race-based violence. These policies, however, do not protect youth who identify as LGBT (lesbian, gay, bisexual, and transgendered).

LGBT students face stigmatization and a significant number of stressors in the school environment, including ostracism, physical violence, and verbal harassment (Jordan, Vaughan, & Woodworth, 1997). Gay and lesbian high school students face more prejudice in school than African-American teen students do, according to a 1999 CBS News poll that surveyed attitudes on the class of 2000 (CBS News, 1999). These feelings are compounded by the indifference of school staff. Derogatory remarks by fellow student directed toward LGBT youth are many times not challenged by teachers, administrators, or counselors, whereas a similar racist statement would likely prompt a reprimand (O'Conor, 1994).

According to Lang and Salas (1998), school districts in Michigan that have attempted to include limited diversity education in the curriculum have not adequately provided for professional development of school staff or engaged students with extracurricular activities that promote inclusion. Without state board policies, adequate resources, and enforcement of these policies, school reform initiatives are difficult to realize.

Student Learning Programs

Student learning programs designed to combat prejudice, stereotypes, and biases emphasize two separate approaches. In the first approach, educators attack the negative behaviors associated with cultural conflict to change cognitive, or belief, systems. They help students change their behavior by instructing them to resist the expression of behaviors associated with prejudice, for example. With this approach, students learn to respond constructively to anger associated with conflict with a different culture. Belief systems change only after students internalize the behavioral changes.

As the discussions of conflict resolution education (Chapter 4) and peer mediation programming (Chapter 5) outline, students learn a process of resolving conflict through win-win scenarios or mediation. Through this systematic process, students tackle the conflicts constructively, by changing their behaviors during conflictual situations. If they use constructive resolution methods consistently, this behavior encourages them to view "others" differently. For example, two students constantly call each other racially inappropriate names during lunch, which ultimately results in conflicts. The two students readily behave this way toward each other, and heightening the conflict is the anger they feel toward each other. A diversity education program would aim to eliminate the name-calling behavior and reduce the anger associated with the situation. These changes in behavior eventually influence the students' way of thinking about each other.

The second approach of student learning programs seeks to change prejudicial behaviors and attitudes by combating the negative belief. The target of both approaches is to change both behavior and beliefs, but while the first approach changes behavior, which then influences beliefs, the second program seeks to change negative beliefs first, which then influences behavior. Once students understand that all people have different beliefs, they can begin to focus on what they have in common. An appropriate model for discussing differences in belief systems appears in Figure 6.1.

Thornton (1997) has transformed the well-known Kluckhohn model for categorizing individual beliefs and values into five categories or orientations (Kluckhohn & Strondtbeck, 1961). According to Thornton, each orientation possesses a range of associated beliefs. For instance, human nature is one orientation in which individuals possess particular belief systems: some individuals believe that human nature is basically good, while others believe that human nature is basically bad. According to the model, others believe that human nature falls somewhere in between, a mixture of both good and evil.

To challenge the prejudicial belief systems students hold, educators must first teach students not to view a belief different from their own as negative and, second, teach them to understand that a particular belief system can promote a specific behavior. Some behaviors people exhibit might be the result of their belief system, which, while different, is not necessarily bad. Using the human nature example, students must learn that beliefs concerning human goodness vary and, therefore, so does behavior. Students who think that human nature is basically good leave their cars,

Figure 6.1   The Kluckhohn Model

The theory of differences in cultural value orientations was first proposed by Kluckhohn (Kluckhohn & Strondtbeck, 1961) and was adapted for purposes of professional education by Thornton (1997).

Orientation	Range				
Human Nature	Basically Evil	Neutral	Mixture of Good and Evil	Basically Good	
	Mutable / Immutable	Neutral / Immutable		Mutable / Immutable	
Man–Nature Relationship	Subjugation to Nature	Harmony with Nature		Mastery over Nature	
Time Sense	Past Oriented (Tradition Bound)	Past Oriented (Situational)		Future Oriented (Goal Bound)	
Activity	Being (Inner Development)	(Expressive/ Emotional) Being-in-Becoming		Doing (Action Oriented)	
Social Relations	Lineality (Authoritarian)	Collaterality (Collective Decisions)		Individualism (Equal Rights)	

homes, and lockers unlocked, while those who believe that human nature is basically bad lock their cars, homes, and lockers securely.

To help students understand this concept, teachers might ask them to offer examples of their experiences confronting a different belief system. For example, nearly everyone has experienced a situation like the one that follows. Two high school friends fight constantly about time. One student drives to school and picks the other up every morning. The second student is always late, and the friend ends up sitting in the driveway waiting. Inevitably, conflict arises between the two. The students' behavior results from differences in their belief systems concerning time. The student who is consistently late is not lazy or stupid but possesses a belief system that conflicts directly with the driver's. Neither belief system is wrong. The key to improving this situation is for both individuals to appreciate the opposing belief system and not view one belief as more correct than the other. Understanding that a continuum of values and belief systems exists and that these values and beliefs influence behavior can promote more positive interactions between individuals whose values and behaviors exist as polar opposites on the continuum.

CONNECTIONS BETWEEN DIVERSITY AND CONFLICT RESOLUTION EDUCATION PROGRAMS

"Through our similarities, we can solve our differences" (Sweeney & Carruthers, 1996, p. 338). This statement accurately reflects the diversity and conflict resolution education program connection. Due to the growing diversity in the student population in schools across America, student differences can be a great source of conflict. Yet, the conflict arising from differences among students can serve as the foundation for conflict participants to create new solutions and learn more about each other and their similarities. Davidman and Davidman (1994) state that the resolution of disputes involving diversity provides students with behaviors and thoughts suited to working and living in a diverse society. Even students from relatively homogenous schools are likely to experience greater diversity after they complete their education in their hometown; therefore, teaching tolerance and acceptance of opposing viewpoints or behaviors prepares them for differences and the accompanying conflicts they will encounter in college and the workplace.

Diversity education programs and conflict resolution education programs fit well with one another because both programs

- teach effective communication skills (see Figure 6.2),
- emphasize the important of perspective taking and understanding multiple points of view,
- urge introspection on individual behaviors both present and past, and
- support collaborative processes through peer dialogue.

Figure 6.2   Communication Skills and Diversity Education

Effective communication skills in schools help empower individuals who feel they have little voice in the school. If these individuals could communicate well, they'd be less likely to express themselves in destructive ways. Effective communication skills allow students to express their discontent with stereotypes, biases, and prejudices that exist in the school and the treatments these students receive in school. Effective student communication also helps school leaders identify behaviors that support stereotypes, biases, and prejudices, which proves invaluable to them in choosing educational programming to decrease such behavior. Conflict resolution education and, specifically, communication skills education then becomes less about conflict resolution and more about creating environments for sharing and understanding others.

Effect of Culture on Communication Skills

Active listening skills are critical components of conflict resolution education (see Chapter 4). Improved active listening skills tend to improve constructive conflict resolution strategies. Cultural factors can influence some aspects of active listening, however. For instance, listeners offer validation, an important listening skill, by means of nonverbal cues, such as head nodding and direct eye contact. Cultural and personal norms that consider direct eye contact unacceptable can deeply affect the success of conflict resolution. When teaching conflict resolution education and active listening skills, it is critical that educators model alternative listening behaviors that de-emphasize direct eye contact but still demonstrate attention to the speaker, such as through hand gestures and body posture.

Educators should try to be aware of other cultural preferences related to conflict resolution techniques; for example, the distance one stands or sits from another to show interest and attention might differ across cultures. Of course, individual differences within cultures can also play a role, making generalizations of cultural preferences impossible. Teachers must also consider *I* messages within a cultural context. Use of *I* messages in a highly authoritarian household or society might be considered very disrespectful. Discomfort can also occur with gender differences and the expression of *I* messages, with women feeling less comfortable with expressing themselves and their needs as compared with men (Franzwa & Lockhart, 1998). In these cases, teachers might still demonstrate *I* messages, but they might focus on voice inflection in the delivery of the message. Other educators might choose to teach active listening skills only.

Communication Skills and Diversity Education

Effective communication skills in schools help empower individuals who feel they have little voice in the school. If these individuals could communicate well, they'd be less likely to express themselves in destructive ways. Effective communication skills allow students to express their discontent with stereotypes, biases, and prejudices that exist in the school and the treatments these students receive in school. Effective student communication also helps school leaders identify behaviors that support stereotypes, biases, and prejudices, which proves invaluable to them in choosing educational programming to decrease such behavior. Conflict resolution education and, specifically, communication skills education then become less about conflict resolution and more about creating environments for sharing and understanding others.

Cyberbullying

Increasingly prevalent in schools, cyberbullying is heightening bias-based violence. Cyberbullying involves the use of technology to support intentional, repeated, and harmful behavior by an individual or group that is intended to harm others. Cases of cyberbullying are being linked to school shootings, gang violence, and even suicide. According to an i-SAFE survey (National i-SAFE Survey, 2004) of 1,500 students in Grades 4 through 8,

- 58 percent of kids admit that someone has said mean or hurtful things to them online. More than 4 out of 10 say it has happened more than once.
- 53 percent of kids admit having said something mean or hurtful to another person online. More than 1 in 3 have done so more than once.
- 35 percent of kids have been threatened online. Nearly 1 in 5 have been threatened more than once.

Examples of bias-based cyberbullying include the following:

- E-mail hacking: "I have this one friend and he's gay and his account got hacked and someone put all these really homophobic stuff on there and posted like a mass bulletin of like some guy with his head smashed open by a car." (Terry, age 14)
- "There's one MySpace from my school this year. There is a boy in my class who everybody hates. . . . And we started this thing, some girl in my class started this I Hate [Name] MySpace thing. So everybody in school goes on it to comment bad things about this boy." (Jessica, age 16)

Kowalski and Limber (2007) suggest the following for educators:

- Educate your students, teachers, and other staff members about cyberbullying, its dangers, and what to do if someone is cyberbullied.
- Be sure that your school's antibullying rules and policies address cyberbullying.
- Closely monitor students' use of computers at school.
- Use filtering and tracking software on all computers, but don't rely solely on this software to screen out cyberbullying and other problematic online behavior.
- Investigate reports of cyberbullying immediately. If cyberbullying occurs through the school district's Internet system, you are obligated to take action.

CONFLICT RESOLUTION STRATEGY SELECTION

The United States has many lawyers, many firearms, highly violent media, and many episodes of youth violence. China has few lawyers, few firearms, highly violent media, and few episodes of youth violence. The fact is, strategies people use to resolve conflicts are culture-specific. Conflict resolution and diversity education must emphasize the fact that cultural differences influence perceptions of conflict resolution strategies and discuss some of the differences in values and expectations of behavior during conflict resolution.

Conflict resolution strategies, such as aggression and negotiation, vary greatly depending on cultural understanding. Different cultures view aggression and behaviors that might be construed as aggressive differently. In Japan, for instance, it is considered highly rude to refuse an offer. In fact, stating a direct "No" to an offer can be interpreted as a hostile gesture, even when the offer is as innocuous as an additional helping of food. Other cultures view rejection of an offer as customary and certainly not an act of aggression. Refusing an additional portion of food in America simply exhibits a full stomach or distaste for the food. In China, pointing the spout of a teapot toward someone is considered challenging and aggressive. In the United States, the direction of a tea spout would have little meaning and certainly would not be perceived as aggressive. The different interpretation of simple behaviors can influence conflict resolution. For example, in a mediation involving an exchange student from Japan and an Hispanic-American student, the Hispanic-American student rejected a proposed agreement by simply stating, "No." The Japanese student stormed out of the room and returned only when the other student apologized and made the assurance that instead of saying, "No," he would say, "Let's think about that later," which essentially meant no but was completely nonthreatening and preferable to the Japanese student.

One's culture also affects perceptions of negotiation. Negotiation is a useful and constructive method of conflict resolution, yet the mechanisms for negotiation differ across cultures. In the United States, negotiation occurs frequently throughout the day: children negotiate with parents over playtime, bedtime, and eating their vegetables, and students negotiate with teachers about due dates of homework. Negotiation is a method individuals use to accommodate differing interests and agendas. Negotiation is a primary tool in competitive (conflictual) situations, but it is also used in cooperative arrangements (students performing a joint task). But not all cultures negotiate in the same way. Negotiation in American society is similar across situations, while in Middle Eastern countries, negotiation strategies, skills, and language differ according to the situation. Arabic has different terms for negotiating with family members, negotiating in the marketplace, and negotiating matters of foreign importance.

While most cultures agree on what are considered constructive and destructive methods of resolving conflict, educators and school leaders have to appreciate that the behaviors associated with constructive versus destructive methods can differ. Cultural differences often play a role in defining the needs of the individual. In the example of the mediation between the Japanese and Hispanic-American student, the student who said, "No," really meant, "No, let's do this instead," but the other student in the mediation heard, "No, that's a stupid idea." To reach an agreement, cultural differences had to be considered.

STRATEGIES FOR
DIVERSITY EDUCATION

As with conflict resolution educational programming, diversity education does not yet have strong consistent support for its use in classrooms across America. The reasons for the lack of empirical support are the changing definition of *diversity* and few consistent, stringent experimental designs among implemented programs. The definition of *diversity education,* which originally emphasized interethnicity, has not expanded to include sensitivity in attitude and behavior toward individuals who are different in a number of ways. What research has been conducted, such as by Campbell and Farrell (1985) and Burnstein (1989), has found that multicultural programming is most effective in fostering more positive attitudes and behaviors when

- all children are involved in the educational training;
- the educational programming is long-term and infused into the curriculum; and
- teachers have the skills, knowledge, and attitudes to support and deliver the education.

Reflection is a critical component for improving student interactions. Before beginning the process of building an inclusive classroom, educators must recognize and acknowledge their affiliation with various groups in society and the advantages and disadvantages of belonging to each group. For example, for White females, membership in the White, middle-class group affords certain privileges in society; at the same time, being a female presents challenges in a male-oriented world. More specifically, teachers need to assess how belonging to one group influences how one relates to, views, and behaves toward other groups.

While little is known about specific successful methods of teaching constructive conflict resolution with diverse student populations, more is known about strategies useful for creating more harmonious environments with students of interracial and interethnic backgrounds.

Gordon Allport's (1954) well-known principles regarding diversity programming have withstood the test of time. Allport concludes that contact under controlled circumstances reduces prejudices, stereotypes, and biases and fosters positive interactions. Most importantly, however, circumstances for positive relations in the classroom must be carefully planned and not assumed to occur merely because students are forced to interact with one another. Allport suggests the following for school leaders:

- Teachers and change agents should support equality in the classroom and during learning situations.
- Teachers and school leaders should emphasize common interests and similar characteristics (as opposed to differences) in the school and classroom.

- Teachers and school leaders should enhance opportunities for students to get to know one another through collaborative learning experiences that require cooperation of group members to reach goals.
- School leaders should promote positive interactions among diverse groups through peer-led activities, recruiting leaders from the diverse groups to promote positive interactions. Likelihood of positive interactions improves when leaders of the various racial or ethnic groups support development of standards or social norms favoring interactions. Schools might create diversity councils made up of student representatives from each racial or ethnic group in the school. The council provides guidance to the school administration on selection of programs to educate (and entertain) students on diversity issues. Once the socially popular students are involved with the activity, social networks that cross ethnic and racial lines occur.

Allport and other researchers recommend that school leaders employ cooperative learning groups and antibias education to encourage constructive conflict resolution and multicultural principles of acceptance and tolerance for students of all races and ethnicities.

Cooperative Learning Groups

Research supports the use of cooperative learning groups with diversity education (Pate, 1988; Rogers, Miller, & Hennigan, 1981; Warring, Johnson, Maruyama, & Johnson, 1985). Cooperative learning groups help build positive interactions among students of different races, ethnicities, genders, and abilities. Research finds that students exposed to cooperative learning on a consistent basis demonstrate greater cross-cultural friendships both in number and depth of relationships and that conflict decreases in classrooms that use cooperative learning activities. Students recognize that they need each other for success and quickly identify strengths and weaknesses of group members to succeed at tasks. Cooperative learning groups also provide students with opportunities to practice effective communication skills, as they must continually share their progress toward achieving the group's goal.

According to an African culture, disputes between individuals in the community are the concern and responsibilities of every member of that tribe (Robarchek, 1997). If a tribe member has knowledge of a conflict between individuals, the tribe has a duty to bring it to the attention of the headman or, in the case of a school setting, a teacher or other administrator. The headman arranges a *becharaa'*, a formal assembly, to resolve the dispute. The headman summons the disputants, their families and supporters, and any interested tribe members to engage in a full discussion and debate of the conflict. The becharaa' can be used to enhance cooperative learning groups and improve the overall classroom climate.

Direct Antibias Education

Antibias education is intended to reduce students' negative stereotypes, biases, and prejudices by improving their ability to understand themselves and others. Antibias educational tools include appropriate and entertaining media, activities that emphasize similarities among students, and activities that develop perspective-taking skills in connection with cooperative learning experiences.

Films, videos, guest speakers, and theatrical productions that emphasize the damage prejudice causes are particularly useful for students in middle and senior high schools. Antibias education programming initiatives often begin with guest speakers presenting true stories of how bias and prejudice have affected their lives or how individuals who demonstrated biased and prejudicial behavior have changed their ways. Films with realistic plots and effective characters are extremely valuable for secondary school students; however, the media message should be subtle, as students in this age group resent being told what to think.

A critical first step for antibias education is engaging students in understanding the wide range of diversity and human characteristics.

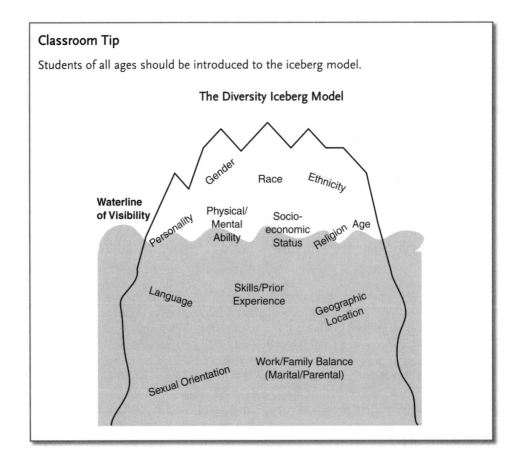

Classroom Tip

Students of all ages should be introduced to the iceberg model.

The Diversity Iceberg Model

Using an adaptation of the iceberg model, educators can introduce the concept of how diversity dimensions above the waterline are things that we often see in a person when we first meet him or her. Those characteristics below the waterline are important yet are difficult to "see." Often, individuals make assumptions about characteristics below the waterline, based on their own experiences, rather than getting to know the other individual in a more personal way. Stereotyping, biases, and discrimination may occur. Educators should talk to students regarding strategies for better understanding the characteristics of a person that are below the waterline. Students should identify their own personal waterline. Is their waterline higher and, therefore, people know few things about them? Or is their waterline lower than that of others—do they feel safer disclosing more information to others?

Establishing the range of diversity dimensions enables students to understand that diversity is broader than race and ethnicity. For secondary students, a reflective analysis on the diversity of their environment is an important additional step. Please see Figure 6.3 for a Cultural Assessment Profile to use with students. The purpose of the Cultural Assessment profile is to provide students with an opportunity to assess their level of interactions with individuals different from themselves. The profile also provides an opportunity for students to question the categories of race/ethnicity; discuss how culturally insular their lives may or may not be; and, if given a choice, discuss whether students elect to interact with others different from themselves. Educators may also wish to complete this profile.

Next, educators should select activities that help students appreciate their similarities and de-emphasize their differences. One of the objectives of diversity training in the schools is to promote acceptance of others' belief systems while learning about or understanding the self in relation to others, as in the maxim "Know thyself, know thy neighbor." Because introspection often leads to acceptance and inclusion of different "others," educators and school leaders should begin antibias education by educating students about themselves. Initially, it is helpful to have students learn more about their own backgrounds—studying family genealogy, interviewing family members about parenting strategies and traditions, and so on—with the goal of discovering the similarities among people.

Circle Game Activity

Teachers might use the circle game to encourage discovery of similarities with students of all ages. In groups of four or five, students draw a circle in the middle of a large piece of paper. They then write or draw in the circle four things common to each of the group members. Answers can be very simple, such as "We all own a dog," or "We all like the color blue." Groups report to the class the similarities only. After students have worked in these groups in cooperative learning activities for four or five weeks,

Figure 6.3 Cultural Assessment Profile

Instructions

In the table below, check the categories that are represented in your environment.

	African/ African American	Arab/ Arab American	Asian/ Asian American	European/ European American	Latino/ Latina	Native American	Other
I am							
In my environment							
My friends are mostly							
Teachers in this school are							
People who work in this school, besides teachers, are							
Students in this school are							
My dentist is							
My doctor is							
People who live in my home are							
People who visit my home are							
People who live near my home are							
People whom I worship with are							

ask students to repeat the exercise, only this time, have them generate four things that are dissimilar.

Verbal and Nonverbal Cues Activity

Another simple classroom exercise is to have students write about the verbal and nonverbal clues they receive from significant adults in their life concerning race, religion, gender, work ethic, family, and the importance of education. When they share these responses, students see similarities that cross cultural boundaries. This exercise also highlights for students the source of attitudes toward certain races, religions, and ethnic groups.

School as a Culture Exercise

Determining the similarities between one's own culture and other cultures is the critical next step. One effective exercise for secondary students is to have them think of their school as a culture. Place students in groups of four or five and ask them, first, to think of the norms of the school and what they would like others to know about their school. Then, have them describe what aspects of the school they would like to change and what they would like to see remain unchanged. The exercise encourages students to think about cultural values and norms and characteristics of a "safe" culture (their own school) and to see that the responses of multiple groups are similar (usually the groups report similar answers to these questions).

Mythodrama Technique

Mythodrama, a technique created in Switzerland (Guggenbühl as cited in Brison, Kottler, & Fisher, 2004), involves telling a story, myth, or legend that indirectly portrays the source of a conflict the student may be experiencing. Students should complete the story as to what might happen if the conflict does not end. Divided into small groups, students will describe their story and unresolved ending. Through such discussions, the students acquire an understanding of how the conflict is experienced by themselves as well as others.

Cultural Connections

The next step in traditional antibias education is to connect the cultures of a variety of students. Topics that generate the most similarities and are most useful in appreciating cultural similarities include the concepts of love, family, learning/knowledge, and spirituality. One technique to connect the cultures of the students is counterstereotyping, providing examples of individuals who do not fit with frequently stated stereotypes, such as African-American hockey players or female-led countries. More beneficial to students, however, is a focus on positive characteristics of entire cultures.

Discussing Differences

Once students feel comfortable discussing their own backgrounds and have identified similarities among themselves and their classmates, discussion about differences among students can occur. Role-playing exercises and simulations are appropriate techniques for demonstrating differences among groups in positive ways. Their purposes are to teach students appropriate skills for handling differences in peer relations and teach them how to interact positively with students who demonstrate differences. Topics of role-play can include a family's dietary limitations, religious practices during holidays, and experience with blended or alternative lifestyle families. Another helpful simulation is to create imaginary "cultures" with a variety of cultural norms. Divide the classroom into two groups, each with a cue card outlining typical behaviors and ways of thinking or speaking for their culture. Have students role-play their cultures. Follow-up questions might include these: What did being in that culture feel like? Did members of the other culture mistreat or misunderstand you? In what ways? What could you do to help the other culture understand your culture better?

Teachers should also select activities that develop perspective-taking skills and thus promote better critical thinking skills and more advanced empathy. Some support exists for the idea that challenging students' critical thinking skills affects their thought process regarding prejudices (Walsh, 1988). For example, the exercise regarding the verbal and nonverbal messages from significant adults challenges students' critical thinking skills. A female student might report that a parent verbalized that boys were better than girls and girls have no need to go to college for they should stay at home when they grow up. The student has probably already challenged that message. The intrapersonal conflict that results when a teacher or other adult challenges a student's thought processes plays a significant role in changing student attitudes (Walsh).

Classroom Activity: Learning About Students

In a county with such distinct cultures, how do you get students to see outside their own perspectives without aggression? How do you give students a different view about themselves and others? Ask students to photograph an image of something that is important in their lives and their communities. Ask students to write about these pictures. The exercise may occur several times during the course of the school year. In many cases, students' priorities will change over the course of the year/semester. Identify the shared priorities of the class, which will become more numerous by the end of the class.

Guidelines for Implementing Diversity Education

The following are techniques for successful integration of diversity education programs and potential pitfalls to avoid.

Positive Techniques

The likelihood of success of diversity education programs increases when school leaders take the following actions:

- Create an environment that uses constructive communication strategies so students feel comfortable reporting destructive behaviors.
- Maintain careful records of racial incidents and trends in attitudes. The student diversity council might provide insight, and the types and focus of bias-motivated incidents reflect school attitudes.
- Consistently provide opportunities for teachers to reflect on their attitudes, stereotypes, and biases. Often, nonprofit organizations, such as the National Conference and the Anti-Defamation League, offer low- or no-cost opportunities for adults to participate in diversity dialogue groups.
- Respond concisely and consistently to incidents that arise concerning diversity issues. Immediately address jokes, graffiti, and demeaning comments regarding gender, race, religion, ethnicity, sexual orientation, and socioeconomic status.
- Provide accurate information about diversity issues, consistently reviewing school curriculum for stereotypical inferences and examples.
- Integrate multicultural education and conflict management skill-building opportunities for parents and school support staff. The training serves as an invaluable resource for students seeking role models outside of the school setting.

Potential Pitfalls to Avoid

The following conditions can undermine a diversity education program:

- *Lack of supportive environment to discuss issues of diversity:* School leaders must determine whether staff has appropriate skills, knowledge, and attitudes to challenge biases and stereotypes and provide professional development if staff falls short. They must examine policies and procedures related to diversity and consider creating a clear policy statement concerning race, ethnicity, religion, gender, and sexual orientation. Student handbooks must clearly define diversity in the above terms and not solely as multiethnic or multiracial incidents. All students and parents must receive a copy of this policy statement and notification of any changes in wording of the statement. The school must outline appropriate behaviors concerning the above categories and certain ramifications if incidents surrounding the above guidelines occur. Schools must review hiring practices to maintain racial, cultural, and gender diversity among staff and review procedures for the handling of bias-motive incidents. The school safety team and the student diversity council might also wish to make recommendations in these cases, or students might want to handle the situation through peer mediation.

- *A tourist approach to diversity education:* An example of this approach is celebrating Mexican heritage day and merely covering food, fashion, and language. Rather, school leaders should consider this approach as an introduction to diversity education, which is then followed by a comprehensive program that highlights Mexican-American struggles in the United States, current policies affecting Mexican Americans, and other related topics.
- *Direct antiprejudice lessons:* Students, particularly secondary students, resent films, plays, or training designed to manipulate the way they think. For the program to be effective, the media message must be subtle, must be age appropriate, and must address the relevant issues present in the school: school leaders should not assume that students will transfer a message on racial biases to incidences of sexual harassment, for example. The message is always best if delivered by individuals who are of the same age for secondary students or by individuals with some credibility, appeal, or authority for younger students.
- *Belief that merely forming interethnic or interracial learning groups promotes positive interactions:* Teachers should first have groups perform a nonacademic task. Once some relationship has formed among group members, then the group can carry out an academic task. If an academic task is immediately assigned to a group whose members have been placed together for the purposes of promoting interethnic harmony and failure occurs, group members might blame the differences among members for the group's failure.
- *Low expectations of students from differing backgrounds:* School leaders should be sure to check staff expectations: student differences can influence teacher expectations of behavior and academic competence. Some schools have a tracking process that correlates teacher's grading with ethnic and racial diversity. Teachers provide the names and grades of students, and an administrator cross-references the race, ethnicity, and gender of the students with their grade averages. To ensure accountability, teachers are not aware of this process. The results help determine if a relationship exists between teacher expectations and grades within the school and whether professional development and further monitoring are necessary. Also, the administration might request teaching portfolios to evaluate differential grading systems and expectations.

MODELS OF EFFECTIVE DIVERSITY EDUCATION PROGRAMS

Resolving Conflict Creatively Program (RCCP)

RCCP is a K–12 initiative sponsored by the Educators for Social Responsibility. Designed to develop emotional, social, and ethical development of children through teaching skills, knowledge, and attitudes in conflict management and intergroup relations, RCCP has been implemented in more than 200 schools across the nation. Initial results from self-evaluation sponsored by the Centers for Disease Control and Prevention demonstrate a significant positive effect on children exposed to the program over a substantial time (Gerberding, 2005, "Adolescent Health").

Responding in Peaceful and Positive Ways (RIPP)

RIPP is an effective model for teaching ethnically diverse student populations in Grade 6. Activities require students to work in small groups, handling differences, clarifying values, dealing with prejudice, and managing anger. Evaluations sponsored by the Centers for Disease Control and Prevention show that RIPP significantly reduces physical fights and incidents of being threatened with a weapon (U.S. Department of Education, 1998).

Students Problem Identification and Resolution (SPIR)

SPIR is a promising new model for Grades 1–12. The program is designed to address violent conflicts among students over racial biases. The program requires implementation with personnel from regional centers. Evaluation data are not currently available for this program.

Facing History and Ourselves (FHAO)

FHAO is a classroom intervention aimed at creating a more humane and informed citizenry in an increasingly diverse society. It is a professional development program for educators that helps them foster the healthy moral development and psychological functioning of their junior and senior high school students (Grades 7–12). The objectives for students are to expand their knowledge of history; improve their critical thinking skills; encourage thinking about their roles in and responsibilities to society and community; and increase their awareness of issues of racism, anti-Semitism, social justice, and democratic participation. Results show significant impacts on intervention group students relative to comparison group students, including increased engagement with issues, decreased fighting behavior, decreased racist attitudes, increased interest in other ethnic groups, and increased relationship maturity (interpersonal understanding, negotiation, and personal meaning).

7

Evaluating School Safety Programs

EVALUATION: A NECESSARY COMPONENT OF SCHOOL SAFETY

Evaluating school safety programs is a critical process for maintaining a safe school. The evaluation process should measure school safety strategy implementation, how well the implemented strategies are received by school stakeholders (administration, faculty, staff, and students), and to what extent the strategies result in a safer learning environment and reduced school-associated violence. The evaluation process is fluid and evolves with school programming, as it serves to validate or redefine programming initiatives.

For example, on evaluation, a school leader learns that teachers' knowledge of conflict resolution concepts has improved as a result of professional development on conflict resolution education. As a result of the student education program, students demonstrate an increased knowledge of conflict resolution concepts and a decline in destructive conflict behaviors in the classroom. However, aggressive behavior during lunch and on the bus to and from the school has not decreased.

These results highlight two critical points related to evaluation of school safety programs. First, the results demonstrate the importance of reviewing and modifying the school safety plan to address the evaluation results. In this case, the review and modification of the safety plan might address how to reduce aggressive behaviors among students during the lunch period and on the bus. Because student conduct improved during class but was unaffected during lunch and on the bus, recommendations for future programming might include professional development for lunchroom staff and bus drivers.

Second, the evaluation results provide support for the effectiveness of implemented programming initiatives. In this example, teachers demonstrated improved knowledge of conflict resolution concepts as a result of the professional development program, and students demonstrated improved knowledge and behavior in the classroom as a result of the student education program. School leaders have evidence, therefore, that these school safety programs are valuable.

As Chapter 2 discusses, the school safety team is often responsible for assessing school safety needs from a micro level (individual student and staff members) to a macro level (school–community partnerships). The school safety team recommends, through a safe school plan, mechanisms for addressing these needs, which include developing and implementing student education programs, changing or creating policies and procedures, building school–community partnerships, and improving the school environment. An evaluation, therefore, assists safe school teams in determining the overall effectiveness and success of the safe school plan, its programs, and its strategies. Evaluation also increases the effectiveness of the management and administration of the plan by demanding accountability from school staff, students, and community members.

The evaluation process documents when the measurable goals and objectives determined by the safe school teams have been reached. If the program strategies fulfill the desired goals, school safety teams may decide to expand the goals and develop additional objectives to meet these new goals. Or if school safety teams determine that the objectives in the safety plan are not helping meet school safety goals, the evaluation can assist the team and school leaders in identifying alternative strategies for achieving the school safety improvement goals.

Patience is required when examining the impact of new and enhanced safety initiatives. Positive changes take time, and program stability is essential to the change process (Cook et al., 2000). Educators and change agents, therefore, need to resist the temptation to shift constantly from program to program.

THE ROLE OF THE EVALUATOR

A critical step in the evaluation process is determining who will be responsible for measuring school safety program and strategy success and whether an inside or outside evaluator will conduct the evaluation. In many cases, school leaders and safety teams seek professional, or outside, assistance with program evaluation, employing evaluation consultants through private consulting organizations or local colleges or universities. School safety teams and the professional consultants often work together closely, as the evaluation must reflect school safety initiatives. Consultants can provide technical help with designing the program evaluation, as well as school safety planning before program implementation, collecting data before and during the program implementation, interpreting evaluation results, and providing recommendations for future programming.

Evidence is unclear whether inside or outside evaluations are of higher technical quality (Rossi, Freeman, & Lipseg, 1999). van de Vall and Bolas (1981) suggest that internal evaluations might have a greater effect on programming because of the utility of the results. Internal evaluators are in a better position to communicate findings and recommend program modifications as compared with outside evaluators, who are unfamiliar with the school organization and personnel. Of course, one threat to the validity of an internal evaluation is that individuals involved with program implementation and development might not be entirely unbiased, might wish to see results that support program development and implementation, and might not interpret or even collect data that refutes their stances.

As a rule of thumb, the evaluator should be familiar not only with methods and concepts involved with program evaluation research but also with school safety issues and the range of interventions used to address school safety objectives. Since evaluation experts are often very costly and few are familiar with the content area of school safety issues, unless schools already employ evaluation experts, school teams should consider conducting an evaluation of the school safety program and strategies on their own.

As with the needs assessment, school safety teams should rely on experienced members of the team to provide assistance with the evaluation. Team members, such as teachers and health and mental health professionals, can be particularly helpful in measuring success, as both groups have experience in general evaluation methods and school safety content, including aggression and prosocial behaviors. These school safety team members can facilitate the evaluation design (methods of data collection), collection of the data, analysis of the data, and interpretion of the results. Manuals to assist school teams in undertaking evaluations are available (Maxfield, 2001; Milstein & Wetterhall, 1999). As well, the Hamilton Fish Institute at The George Washington University (www.hamfish.org) possesses a large number of instruments that can be used to measure school climate and safety and student beliefs, among other variables. Selecting valid and reliable instruments is an important step toward completion of a meaningful evaluation process.

Team members with experience might do some of the evaluation themselves; more often, however, they facilitate the data collection process by delegating tasks to school faculty members. For instance, if the safety team determines that data on student behavior in the classroom are necessary, team members ask teachers to observe children's behavior, in a standardized fashion, or to proctor and collect surveys completed by students. Teachers in the school might have either a limited or extremely involved role in the evaluation process. In schools with limited resources, safety team members can help garner support for teachers' involvement with data collection. If teachers choose not to participate in the data collection process, safety team members might recruit volunteers from the community who can be trained in the necessary observational skills and administration of required surveys.

WHAT SHOULD THE EVALUATION MEASURE?

Evaluations must determine if goals and objectives created in the school safety plan for each of the four school safety improvement areas—student education, policies and procedures, school–community partnerships, and the school environment—have been achieved. Therefore, the first critical component in the evaluation process is to identify what kinds of data to collect to measure success. The second critical component is to determine the guidelines that school leaders and safety teams will use to define success.

Evaluating Student Education Programs

Evaluating the success of school safety student education programs is an extremely difficult task, and the concept is not without a great deal of controversy. Due to the paucity of previous empirical studies conducted on student education programs, particularly violence prevention programs, a number of relevant issues concerning student education programs remain unclear. Unlike evaluating student achievement in an academic content area, the measurement of student success in character education, conflict resolution education, and diversity education is difficult because of inconsistent research findings outlining expected student outcomes and the lack of standardized measures available to evaluate success. In cases of evaluating conflict resolution education success, researchers can neither agree on nor clearly define what student outcomes to measure or how to measure student outcomes.

For example, student outcome measures of the effectiveness of conflict resolution education might include (a) a decrease in aggressive behaviors; (b) an increase in prosocial behaviors; (c) a decrease in suspensions, detentions, or expulsions; or (d) knowledge of conflict resolution concepts and vocabulary. Unfortunately, it is unknown how or even whether these outcome measures are ultimately related to safe schools. In addition, empirically tested and standardized measures for assessing changes in aggressive behaviors, prosocial behaviors, and knowledge of conflict resolution concepts and vocabulary are not yet available. For example, how does one define *aggression* when measuring aggressive behaviors? Is the act defined as aggressive if it is physical (more common among males), or should relational conflict involving gossiping or group exclusion (more common among females) be considered aggressive also?

Although consistent and generalizable methods for evaluating school safety student education programs are not currently available, a number of strategies are useful for obtaining some sense of the success of these programs. Quantification of changes in individuals' knowledge, skills, and attitudes can help determine the effectiveness of student education programs involving character education, conflict resolution education, or diversity education. Measuring changes in skills provides evidence that students have developed abilities to demonstrate new ways of behaving during conflict situations, morally challenging situations, and interactions with diverse individuals. Measuring changes in knowledge provides evidence that students have learned relevant vocabulary and concepts related to constructive conflict resolution, moral thought, and diversity. Measuring positive changes in students' attitudes provides evidence that students have modified their thoughts about constructive conflict resolution methods and have developed more sophisticated moral thought and sensitivity toward others.

An evaluation of the effectiveness of student education initiatives in conflict resolution education, character education, and diversity education should seek data on the specific content issues outlined in Figure 7.1 for the three program areas of students' knowledge, skills, and attitudes. They should be measured before student exposure to the training program, during the program, and at a designated time, such as six months, after program implementation.

One method for assessing changes in student knowledge and skills of constructive conflict resolution principles is based in the perspective-taking model of Robert Selman (1981). As Chapter 4 describes, students' ability to take others' perspectives develops over time. However, students often display less sophisticated perspective-taking skill than they are capable of cognitively. Since perspective taking is a socio-cognitive skill that influences selection of a conflict resolution strategy, measurement of this skill provides some evidence of the effectiveness of the conflict resolution education.

Evaluators might compare the level of perspective-taking ability before program implementation and after program exposure. Through an interview or questionnaire, students might review a hypothetical situation and answer several open-ended questions regarding the situation, such as the following:

- What is the problem?
- How does each of the disputants feel?

Figure 7.1   Guide to Evaluation

An evaluation of the effectiveness of student education initiatives in conflict resolution education, character education, and diversity education should seek data on the specific content issues outlined below in the three program areas of students' knowledge, skills, and attitudes.

Student Education	Conflict Resolution Education	Character Education	Diversity Education
Knowledge	Vocabulary and concepts Active listening/ I messages Win-win solutions Mediation and the process	Vocabulary and concepts Moral thought processes Preconventional/ conventional/ postconventional thought	Vocabulary and concepts Prejudice, stereotyping, and biases Kluckhohn model/beliefs
Skills	Demonstrate constructive conflict resolution behaviors, sophisticated perspective-taking abilities, use of active listening// messages	Demonstrate sophisticated levels of moral thought in hypothetical and real morally challenging situations; demonstrate respect, responsibility, and empathy	Demonstrate acceptance, empathy, sensitivity toward others; introspection in group segregation; relationship to others
Attitudes	Motivation to think and behave in peaceful ways	Motivation to think and behave in respectful and responsible ways	Motivation to think and behave in accepting and sensitive ways

- What are some ways to resolve the problem?
- What is the best way to resolve the problem? (While there is not necessarily only one correct answer, this question always elicits a more sophisticated response.)

Evaluators can chart changes in perspective-taking abilities using the Selman (1981) interpersonal negotiation strategy model (Figure 4.1). Students' responses will demonstrate highly egocentric/impulsive resolutions (Levels 0 and 1) or highly sophisticated/collaborative responses (Levels 2 and 3). An evaluation can also assess success of the conflict resolution education program by charting the levels of improvement (or absolute increase of levels) (Barton, 2000) or the number of students performing at or above their cognitive capability. Evaluators can use the Selman model to compare students' level of functioning for perspective taking and constructive conflict resolution skills with the developmental appropriateness of student behavior. Hypothetically, an evaluation might determine that approximately 30 percent of secondary students performed at Levels 0 and 1 (below cognitive appropriateness for their age) before program implementation while only 10 percent performed at this same level after program exposure, which validated program success. For additional assistance in using the Selman model as an assessment tool, refer to Selman, Jaquette, and Bruss-Saunders (1979).

A preliminary analysis of the Children's Constructive Conflict Resolution Scale (CCCRS) may also be useful in determining students' conflict resolution skills (Secor, 1997) before and after program implementation. The survey evaluates social problem-solving, perspective-taking, and compromising skills.

An additional method for determining program effectiveness on students' conflict resolution skills is through student observation. Teachers select a random sample of students, then observe changes in skills demonstrated during interpersonal conflict situations. Observations can provide accurate, detailed information. Data collection is most useful if the evaluators clearly classify and define the types of behaviors they are observing. For instance, evaluators interested in recording the number of physically aggressive behaviors occurring among students during lunch must clearly define *physically aggressive behaviors:* the definition might include pushing, shoving, and hitting but not stealing balls or other play items or assaulting verbally. Observers record the frequency, magnitude, and duration of the behaviors.

One such tool used to evaluate student education programs and, specifically, to collect observational data is the social interaction system (Neckerman, Asher, & Pavlidis, 1994). Trained observers can use this instrument to record defined student behaviors in categories such as prosocial, neutral, verbal negative, and physical negative. This observation system provides evaluators with a useful means of measuring altruistic and sharing behaviors (prosocial); nonassaultive, nonthreatening, nonaltruistic behaviors (neutral); and aggressive verbal and physical behaviors (verbal negative and physical negative) (Grossman et al., 1997). Because the tool uses specifically defined categories of behavior, it clearly measures changes in student skills after exposure to student education programs. Evaluators count the number of times students demonstrate these behaviors. As a rule of thumb, evaluators often use an approximate 20 percent change in demonstrated behavior as a measure of success. For example, if an evaluator finds that a pre- and postintervention comparison demonstrates a 20 percent increase in prosocial behaviors among students and 25 percent decrease in physical and verbal negative behaviors among students, these findings indicate a successful program.

Teachers can also assist with the collection of data designed to establish program effectiveness through teacher rating scales. Surveys are available that ask teachers to evaluate students' behaviors in the classroom and outside of class on the playground and in the lunchroom. Two of the best surveys for assessing school safety interventions are the School Social Behavior Scales (SSBS) and the Achenbach Teacher Report Form (TRF). Parents can complete the Achenbach Child Behavior Checklist (CBCL) (Achenbach, 1994) to determine changes of student behavior in the home.

Evaluations of attitude changes that occur after program implementation are difficult to measure, particularly because students are not always likely to respond truthfully to questions that measure socially undesirable behavior. School leaders may consider using the Normative Orientation to Beliefs about Aggression Scale (NOBAGS) for students in elementary and middle school grades. This 20-item scale developed by Huesmann, Guerra, and Zelli (1994) measures a student's perception on the acceptability of aggressive responses in hypothetical situations. In addition, the Verbal Aggressiveness Scale created by Infante and Wigley (1986) may be useful to measure secondary students' predisposition for verbal aggressiveness.

When evaluating attitudinal change, school leaders may wish to consider a number of online survey tools that ensure anonymity. Tools available through Zoomerang or Survey Monkey are economical to use, particularly for large numbers of participants. In addition, reports are generated through these tools, which makes the data analysis for forced-choice style questions easy to complete.

Data collected from school reports are also necessary in measuring the effectiveness of school safety intervention. However, unlike evaluations that identify changes in individual students, school evaluations provide general information through incident records, disciplinary referrals, and numbers and types of mediations. School safety team members and school leaders should work together to determine their definition of *success* regarding aggregate school data, as definitions depend on individual school factors and, thus, vary by school. Often, schools consider decrements in incident reports along with the numbers of mediations as useful indices of program success. Law enforcement representatives on the school safety team can assist with school data collection by providing statistics of juvenile crime in and around the school campus before and after programming.

Measuring the quality of school safety program delivery is critical to identifying program success, as the level of instruction can influence student outcomes. Evaluation should attempt to determine how well faculty members present student learning programs, facilitate follow-up discussion, and engage students in role-play exercises to improve skills. Methods might include observing the peer or school safety team, correlating student performance to teacher, evaluating examples of student work, and so on.

Evaluating Policies and Procedures

In general, evaluating the success of policies and procedures regarding school safety is much easier than evaluating the success of student learning programs. Data that school leaders and school staff collect should be suffi-cient to determine if school policies and procedures accurately address the needs of the students and the school community and how well policies and procedures have been communicated to students, staff, and parents. Data should reflect whether school safety issues arose where policies and procedures were not available or were incomplete or whether they were inappropriately written to handle the situation. Informal telephone sur-veys of parents concerning knowledge of policies and procedures and written surveys of students and teachers are two methods of collecting this information.

For example, a school safety team assessed the school needs and deter-mined that the school needed a crisis response plan to handle evacuation of the student body. A response plan was created, school faculty was informed of the plan, and the plan was executed during a crisis response drill. Students were evacuated properly, yet crisis support from law enforcement never showed at the scene. Revisiting the crisis response policy and proce-dures, evaluators found that no provisions were made to contact local law enforcement.

Evaluations can highlight when policies and procedures do not appro-priately address all possible school safety issues. For instance, a school might have a zero-tolerance policy concerning student assaults, with mandatory suspensions of 30 or 45 days, but the policy does not outline where students will be during this suspension (home, alternative school sites, in-school sus-pension) and whether certified teachers will be available for these students.

Evaluating School–Community Partnerships

In measuring the success of school–community partnerships, evalua-tors should consider collecting data beyond that concerning the number and type of partnerships involved in the school safety plan. They should also answer the following questions:

- Describe the new partnerships formed as a result of the school safety program and the partnerships that evolved (from previous school involvement) as a result of the school safety program.
- Describe the nature of the partnership involvement, including the frequency with which the partners interact and the services the part-ners provide.
- Describe the level of satisfaction of the partners. Are interactions enjoyable?
- Does the program coordinate effectively among all partners, or does further outreach need to occur?

In the case of evaluating school–community partnerships, qualitative rather than quantitative data might be most useful. Qualitative data, collected through an interview format, provides valuable information as to the usefulness and satisfaction of school–community partnerships and whether additional support is necessary for reaping the greatest benefits of partnerships.

Evaluating the Environment

Similar to the evaluation of the other school improvement areas, the evaluation of the school environment must measure the success of the proposed goals and objectives of the school safety plan and determine to what degree the environment is safer through the plan's goals and objectives.

For example, a school safety team developed a goal of restricting passage in the school by both students and visitors, with objectives of limiting entrance and exit to two school doors, providing all students and school staff with identification badges, and creating policies limiting parent access to the school during specified visiting hours. Data collected during the day regarding hallway passage should assist school safety team members in determining if program objectives successfully reduced hallway traffic and unidentified hallway walkers.

The 2008 School Safety Index Self-Assessment Tool can be used for purposes of collecting baseline data in the assessment stage and for outcome data collection after strategy implementation. Upon completion of the 12-question tool, leaders receive an instant score showing how their school or district compares to the national school safety average. Using the self-assessment tool, school leaders, parents, and policy makers learn about the physical and cyber safety of their school. Each question highlights an indicator of strong school safety programs.

School leaders might measure student and staff perceptions of the school climate using the Hoy's Organizational Health Inventory (OHI-E). This instrument is useful for teachers and can be adapted for students of different educational levels (Hoy & Feldman, 1987). Another example of a tool that measures school climate is included in Figure 7.2.

MECHANISMS FOR EVALUATING SCHOOL SAFETY PROGRAMS

School leaders and the school safety team must consider how to measure the success of school safety programs and strategies. Should program and strategy success be measured based on the effectiveness of the delivery of the program, or should success be determined by the impact of the program and strategies on the targeted participants (students)? School safety teams should be interested in measuring both the delivery of the program and the impact of the program and strategies on student outcomes.

Figure 7.2   Secondary Student–School Climate Instrument

We are interested in learning how you feel about your school. Please read each question and circle the answer that best describes how you feel most of the time. The survey is anonymous, so no one will know how you answer.

Teacher: _____
Grade: _____   Date: _____

1. I think that my school is safe.

1	2	3	4	5
Strongly disagree	Disagree	Somewhat agree	Agree	Strongly agree

2. I feel safe in my classroom.

1	2	3	4	5
Strongly disagree	Disagree	Somewhat agree	Agree	Strongly agree

3. I feel safe in the hallway.

1	2	3	4	5
Strongly disagree	Disagree	Somewhat agree	Agree	Strongly agree

4. I feel safe in the cafeteria.

1	2	3	4	5
Strongly disagree	Disagree	Somewhat agree	Agree	Strongly agree

5. I feel safe on the playground.

1	2	3	4	5
Strongly disagree	Disagree	Somewhat agree	Agree	Strongly agree

6. I witness violence in school.

1	2	3	4
Never	Sometimes	Often	Every day
	(1–2 times/month)	(1–2 times/week)	

7. I witness violence in my classroom.

1	2	3	4
Never	Sometimes	Often	Every day

8. I witness violence on the school grounds.

1	2	3	4
Never	Sometimes	Often	Every day

9. How do adults react to violence?

   a. They do nothing.
   b. They stop the students and punish the participants.
   c. They stop the violence and try to talk out a solution.
   d. They stop the violence but then walk away.
   e. Other: _____

10. How do you react to school violence?

   a. I do nothing.
   b. I join the crowd.
   c. I stop the participants and try to talk out a solution.
   d. I stop the violence but then walk away.
   e. Other: _____

(Continued)

Figure 7.2 (Continued)

11. What are some things that will stop violence in your school? (Circle as many answers as you wish.)
     a. Teach ways to handle violence.
     b. Have more adults on school grounds, in the cafeteria, and hallways.
     c. Create strict punishments.
     d. Talk about cooperation and violence prevention.
     e. Other: _____

12. How often have you been a victim of violence and/or bullied?

1	2	3	4
Never	Sometimes	Often	Every day

13. How often do you engage in violence against others?

1	2	3	4
Never	Sometimes	Often	Every day

14. Please read each of the following statements and indicate your perceptions about the inclusiveness of your school.

1	2	3	4	5	N/A
Strongly agree	Agree	Neutral	Disagree	Strongly disagree	

Students treat each other with respect at your school.

1   2   3   4   5

Students respect religious differences at your school.

1   2   3   4   5

Students at this school respect racial and ethnic differences.

1   2   3   4   5

Students are respectful of people's sexual orientation (lesbian, gay, heterosexual, bisexual, transgendered) at your school.

1   2   3   4   5

Male students are respectful of female students.

1   2   3   4   5

Students are respectful of people with disabilities at this school.

1   2   3   4   5

Students respect others from different socioeconomic status levels.

1   2   3   4   5

Students feel safe at school.

1   2   3   4   5

Students feel that school is inclusive.

1   2   3   4   5

15. Please describe an experience in your school that you perceive as bias-based conflict and/or violence? How was the situation handled?

Process Evaluation Versus
Outcome and Impact Evaluation

Three kinds of evaluation processes are useful in demonstrating school safety success: the process evaluation, the outcome evaluation, and the impact evaluation. The following discussion combines outcome and impact evaluations and compares them with process evaluation. For the most comprehensive evaluation of school safety programming, evaluators should measure success through both a process and an outcome-impact evaluation.

Process Evaluation

A process evaluation describes and assesses the quality of implementation activities. It determines the effectiveness of the operations or delivery of a program. For example, school leaders who have implemented a peer mediation program can use process evaluation to assess whether the mediation times and program administration are successful.

Process evaluations can also determine whether a program is reaching its intended audience. For example, the safe school plan identifies that a curriculum process approach to conflict resolution education is the best approach to reduce violent conflict in the classroom. The safe school plan recommends use of a curriculum for Grades 1 through 3. The teachers receive no professional development on the curriculum. In this case, a process evaluation would measure teachers' accurate implementation of the program. A process evaluation might involve observation of teaching methods or a review of student homework to determine whether program delivery is standardized and valuable to students or whether the curriculum is not useful for students and professional development opportunities might improve implementation.

Common process evaluation questions include the following:

- How many students are involved in the program/strategy?
- Are these students the intended participants?
- Do they receive the appropriate amount, type, and quality of program/ strategy?
- Is staffing adequate in number and level of competence to deliver the services?
- Are adequate resources available to support the program/strategy?

Outcome-Impact Evaluation

Results of the process evaluation can affect results of the outcome and impact evaluation. Compared with the process evaluation, which evaluates the quality of the delivery of the program, the outcome-impact evaluation demonstrates the effect of the delivery on student variables. The outcome evaluation studies the immediate effects of a school safety program/strategy intervention, and an impact evaluation assesses long-term effects of an intervention. For instance, evaluators wishing to determine whether individual skills, knowledge, and attitude have changed as a result of program intervention would use the outcome-impact evaluation to measure these individual characteristics.

Using the example above of students in Grades 1 through 3 exposed to a standardized conflict resolution education curriculum, an outcome-impact evaluation would measure the influence of the program on variables such as constructive conflict resolution skills, knowledge, and attitudes. This type of evaluation is most useful in comparing levels of skills, knowledge, and attitudes before and after program (or curriculum) exposure. Differences that occur after school safety initiatives as compared with initial or baseline levels serve as the measure of success.

Successful outcome and impact evaluation measures usually include multiple assessments (before, during, and after implementation) of student variables. To determine the long-term effects of a program implemented for an entire school year, the impact evaluation of student variables should take place two to three weeks after intervention, two to three months after intervention, and six to eight months after intervention. Baseline data compared with data at these intervals provide information regarding changes in specific behaviors or skills over the course of the intervention. The evaluations should remain as similar as possible, although evaluators can change the order of questions on a survey or questionnaire to prevent practice effects. When the assessment has students respond to questions about hypothetical situations to measure perspective taking and moral thought, the situations should change, but the questions can remain the same. Any of the methods described earlier in the chapter are useful for impact evaluations, including observing student behavior, use of the Selman model, and collection of data on school incidents and number of mediations. Simple before- and after-program evaluation is the most effective method for measuring school safety program success, particularly with regard to student learning outcomes.

The simple before-and-after evaluation method isn't useful unless all students are exposed to programs for the same period or all schools in a district implement programs at the same time. Also, if the school implements multiple programs, the simple before and after evaluation method might not be as useful. For instance, a school implements a peer mediation program and a diversity education program to reduce intercultural conflict in the school. An outcome-impact evaluation measures skills, knowledge, and attitudes before program implementation and after program exposure. No differences occur among students. Are the diversity and peer mediation programs unsuccessful? Possibly, the mediation program or the diversity program alone would have produced measurable impact on students, yet combined, the programs were not effective.

In this case, use of a more traditional experimental design might have been better. In an experimental design, random assignment to experimental manipulation (an independent variable) and a control group occurs. Generally, if improvements are greater in the intervention group than in the control group, then the intervention is considered a success. To achieve reliable data in the example above, schools in the district might have had to impose several conditions. For example, one school might implement only peer mediation, one school only diversity education, one school both peer mediation and diversity education, and one school no programming at all to serve as the control. (This example compares programming in schools rather than classrooms because positive programming effects may carry over to nonintervention classrooms, which mask the real effects of the program.)

Although the true experimental design may provide more causal linkage between program implementation and measurable outcomes, it is more difficult to conduct within a single school. Students exposed to the program in one classroom might use the skills they've learned in a nonintervention classroom, which compromises the control situation. Hence, the before-and-after method of program evaluation is most useful.

Evaluating school safety initiatives is critical to maintaining safer school environments. Through the evaluation process, school leaders better understand what programming initiatives are effective or what initiatives need modification. This review process validates the important work of the school safety team members and demonstrates support of school safety as a priority in the daily operation of the school.

Appendix A

*Sample School Safety Handbook
Table of Contents and General
Emergency Management Plan*

The table of contents from the School Safety Handbook and the General Emergency Management Plan that follow are draft documents from School District U-46, Elgin, Illinois. (Used with permission.)

SAFETY HANDBOOK TABLE OF CONTENTS

Off-Campus

Environmental Hazard

Chemical Fallout

Hazardous Spill

Air Pollutants

Explosions, Fire, Plane Crash

Gas Leaks

Hostage Incident

Loss of Utilities

School Bus Accident

Weapons on Campus

Weather Related

Earthquake

Snowstorm

Flood

Storm Conditions

Tornado/Lightning

Fire Drill

GENERAL EMERGENCY MANAGEMENT PLAN

When a situation is identified and verified as potentially life threatening, the Principal declares that the emergency plan will be implemented.

Phase I

The Emergency Management Team members report to the Principal's conference room or communicate via walkie-talkies, are briefed, and assume predetermined duties.

Person Responsible	*Function*
Principal	Announce emergency over public address system.
	Contact Area Superintendent.
	Contact School Community Relations Office.
Head Custodian	Secure building.
Principal's Secretary	Turn off bell system.
	Maintain log of notifications, events, and times.
	Inform receptionist of appropriate public information.
AP 12	Meet Police/Fire.
AP 10	Designate deans' assistants to sweep the building to search for students not under supervision and place in supervised room, check for outsiders, and maintain control of hallways.
Dean	Deal with parent issues.
Area Superintendent	Inform and update Superintendent.
All staff	No child shall be released to parent until the "all clear" signal is given.

Phase II

Initial action has been taken—Phase II occurs immediately after crisis.

Person Responsible	*Function*
Principal	Declare "all clear" after consultation with investigating officers.
	Update Administrative/Emergency Team.

	Inform staff of time of voluntary staff meeting(s).
	Meet with press.
Area Superintendent	Update Superintendent.
Director of School Community Relations	Prepare press release.
AP12	Calculate changes to the class period schedule for announcement to staff.
Director of Guidance	Activate Crisis Team if appropriate.
Administrative Team	Meet after voluntary staff meeting to formulate subsequent plans.
	Prepare statement of updated information to be placed in each staff member's mailbox between voluntary staff meetings.

Phase III

Action to deal with aftermath

Person Responsible	*Function*
Principal	Conduct meeting with Emergency Team to review any new information.
	Conduct voluntary morning staff meeting if appropriate.
	With Area Superintendent, decide on need to hold an informational parent meeting. It would be conducted by implementing the Board of Education meeting format and include a representative from the Office of the Chief of Police as appropriate.
Director of School Community Relations	Publicize a parent meeting.

Appendix B

*Sample School Safety
Information Policy Agreement*

SCHOOL SAFETY INFORMATION POLICY AGREEMENT:

_____ SCHOOL DISTRICT

Statement of Intent

The parties to this agreement are committed to maintaining a safe school environment. We acknowledge and agree that school safety will be enhanced through the effective sharing of information and resources. The goal of this agreement is to establish procedures to follow when an incident defined in the School Safety Response Guide section of the Statewide School Safety Information Policy occurs. The parties further agree to develop internal policies and cooperative procedures as needed to implement the local School Safety Information Policy.

We each agree to

1. promote a coordinated effort among agencies and staff to achieve maximum public safety with the goal of reducing juvenile crime.

2. participate in interagency planning meetings, as appropriate.

3. jointly plan, and provide information and access to, training opportunities, when feasible.

4. develop internal policies and cooperative procedures, as needed, to implement this policy and the Statewide Safety Information policy.

5. comply with relevant state and federal law and other applicable local rules that relate to records use, security, dissemination, and retention and destruction.

The School agrees to

1. designate a contact person responsible for receiving information from law enforcement, prosecutors, and courts and inform all parties of the school's designee.

2. notify the pupil's principal of information from law enforcement, prosecutors, or the court system within 24 hours. The principal, within 24 hours of such notice, shall provide such information to relevant building personnel.

3. notify the appropriate law enforcement agency when an adult or a student commits any of the offenses listed in the School Safety Response Guide on school property, on school-sponsored transportation, or at school-sponsored activities.

4. develop appropriate internal written policies to ensure that confidential criminal history information is disseminated only to appropriate school personnel.

Each Law Enforcement Agency agrees to

1. designate a contact person responsible for forwarding information to the designated school personnel and inform all parties of the law enforcement's designee.

2. notify the superintendent, or designee, of crimes committed on school property. Notification shall occur within 24 hours or the next business day when school is in session and shall include the details of the crime committed. Notification shall be within 7 days during the summer. A law enforcement agency may delay reporting of crimes to a school district if such report may compromise an ongoing investigation.

3. notify the superintendent, or designee, promptly of crimes committed off school property that they have reason to believe may pose a significant threat of imminent danger to students, staff, or school property.

The Prosecuting Attorney agrees to

1. designate a contact person responsible for forwarding information to the designated school personnel and inform all parties of the prosecuting attorney's designee.

2. notify the superintendent or designee of any criminal or juvenile court action initiated or taken against a pupil of the school district, including, but not limited to, convictions, adjudications, and dispositions.

This notification shall be initiated within 24 hours after the charge is made when school is in session and include the details of that charge.

3. inquire of each school-aged individual involved in a court action described in this subsection whether the individual is a pupil of a school district and, if so, in which school district.

4. attempt to notify the school district superintendent or the superintendent of the intermediate school district where the pupil attends if it is determined that the individual is a pupil in a school district not located within the county.

The Court agrees to

1. designate a contact person responsible for forwarding information to the designated school personnel and inform all parties of the court's designee.

2. notify the superintendent, or designee, of the name of the individual assigned to monitor a convicted or adjudicated youth attending a public school and how to contact that individual.

Signed this _____day of _____ 2009

Appendix C

Resources

Organizations

Association for Conflict Resolution, 5151 Wisconsin Ave. NW, Suite 500, Washington, DC 20016; (202) 464-9700, (212) 464-9720 fax

Center for Peace and Conflict Studies, Wayne State University, 2320 Faculty Administration Building, Detroit, MI 48202; (313) 577-3453, (313) 577-8269 fax

Children's Creative Response to Conflict, P.O. Box 271, Nyack, NY 10960; (914) 353-1796, (914) 358-4924 fax

CRU Institute, 2330 130th Ave. NE, Building C, Suite 102, Bellevue, WA 98005; (425) 869-4041, 800-922-1988.

Educators for Social Responsibility, 23 Garden St., Cambridge, MA 02138; (617) 492-1764, (617) 864-5164 fax

Harvard Negotiation Project, 500 Pound Hall, Harvard Law School, Cambridge, MA 02138; (617) 495-1684, (617) 495-7818 fax

Ohio Commission on Dispute Resolution and Conflict Management, 77 S. High St., 24th floor, Columbus, OH 43266; (614) 752-9595, (614) 752-9682 fax

Program for Young Negotiators, 20 University Road, Cambridge, MA 02138; 888-832-2479, (617) 354-8467 fax

Resolving Conflict Creatively Program, 163 Third Ave., P.O. Box 103, New York, NY 10003; (212) 387-0225, (212) 387-0510

Curriculum Resources

Anti-Bias Curriculum: Tools for Empowering Young Children (1989), Louise Derman-Sparks & the ABC Task Force, National Association for the Education of Young Children, 1509 16th St. NW, Washington, DC 20036; (202) 232-8777

Campus Alternative Dispute Resolution Clearinghouse; http://www.campus-adr.org

Circles of Learning: Cooperation in the Classroom, 5th ed. (1993), David W. Johnson, Robert T. Johnson, & Edythe Holuhec, Interaction Book Company, 7208 Cornelia Dr., Edina, MN 55435; (612) 831-9500

Conflict Managers Training Manual for Grades 3–6 (1995), Community Board Program Inc., 1540 Market St., Suite 490, San Francisco, CA 94102; (415) 552-1250

Conflict Resolution: An Elementary School Curriculum (1990), Community Board Program Inc., 1540 Market St., Suite 490, San Francisco, CA 94102; (415) 552-1250

Conflict Resolution in the Middle School (1994), William Kreidler, Educators for Social Responsibility, 23 Garden St., Cambridge, MA 02138; (617) 492-1764

Conflict Resolution in the Schools: A Manual for Educators (1996), National Institute for Dispute Resolution, 1726 M St. NW, Suite 500, Washington, DC 20036; (202) 466-4764

Creating the Peaceable School: A Comprehensive Program for Teaching Conflict Resolution (2003), Richard J. Bodine, Donna K. Crawford, and Fred Schrumpf, Research Press, P.O. Box 9177, Champaign, IL 61826; (217) 352-3273

Creative Conflict Resolution: More Than 200 Activities for Keeping Peace in the Classroom, K–6, 2nd ed. (2005), William J. Kreidler, Good Year Books, P.O. Box 91858, Tucson, AZ 85752; (520) 547-2462, 888-511-1530, 888-511-1501 fax

Dealing With Anger: A Video-Based Violence Prevention Program for African-American Youth (1991), W. Rodney Hammond and Vernessa Gipson, Research Press, P.O. Box 9177, Champaign, IL 61826; (217) 352-3273

Friendly Classroom for a Small Planet: A Handbook on a Creative Approach to Living and Problem Solving for Children (1988), P. Prutzman, L. Stern, M. Burger, & G. Bodenhammer, Children's Creative Response to Conflict, P.O. Box 271, Nyack, NY 10960; (914) 353-1796

Giraffe Classroom (1990), Nancy Sokol Green, Center for Non-Violent Communication, 3468 Meadowbrook Blvd., Cleveland Heights, OH 44118; (216) 371-1123

Lessons in Conflict Resolution for Grades 4–6 (1994), New Mexico Center for Dispute Resolution, 620 Roma NW, Suite B, Albuquerque, NM 87102; 800-249-6884

Life Negotiations: The PYN Curriculum for Middle Schools (1996). Jared Curhan, Program for Young Negotiators, 20 University Road, Cambridge, MA 02138; 888-832-2479

Oh, My Manners! (2008), Kingberry Productions Inc., 4463 Barchester Dr., Bloomfield Hills, MI 48302; (248) 594-3811; Kingberry3@aol.com

Peer Mediation: Conflict Resolution in Schools—Program Guide, rev. ed. (1997). Fred Schrumpf, Donna K. Crawford, and Richard J. Bodine, Research Press, P.O. Box 9177, Champaign, IL 61826; (217) 352-3273

Second Step: A Violence Prevention Curriculum, Grades PreK–K/Grades 1–3/Grades 4–5/ Grades 6–8 (1992), Kathy Beland, Committee for Children, 172 20th Ave., Seattle, WA 98122; 800-634-4449

Students Resolving Conflict: Peer Mediation in Schools (1995), R. Cohen and Scott Foresman, 1900 East Lake Ave., Glenview, IL 60025; 800-552-2259

Teaching Young Children in Violent Times (1994), Diane Levin, Educators for Social Responsibility, 23 Garden St., Cambridge, MA 02138; 800-370-2515

Violence: Dealing With Anger (1994), Thomas Crum, Center Communication, 1800 30th St., No. 207, Boulder, CO 80301; (303) 444-1166

Violence Prevention Curriculum for Adolescents (1987), Deborah Prothrow-Stith, Education Development Center Inc., 55 Chapel St., Newton, MA 02160; (617) 969-7100

References

Achenbach, T. (1994). Child behavior checklist and related instruments. In M. E. Maruish (Ed.), *The use of psychological testing for treatment planning and outcome assessment* (pp. 517–549). Hillsdale, NJ: Lawrence Erlbaum.

Allport, G. (1954). *The nature of prejudice.* Reading, MA: Addison-Wesley.

Baer, J. (1976). *How to be an assertive (not aggressive) woman in life, in love, and on the job.* New York: The New American Library.

Bandura, A. (1973). *Aggression: A social learning analysis.* Englewood Cliffs, NJ: Prentice-Hall.

Bandura, A. (1985). *Social foundations of thought and action: A social cognitive theory.* Englewood Cliffs, NJ: Prentice-Hall.

Banks, J. (1994). *An introduction to multicultural education.* Boston: Allyn & Bacon.

Barton, E. A. (2000). *Social-cognitive skill development following a peer mediation program.* Manuscript submitted for publication.

Barton, E. A. (2006). *Bully prevention: Tips and strategies for school leaders and classroom teachers.* Thousand Oaks, CA: Corwin.

Battistich, V., Solomon, D., Watson, M., & Schaps, E. (1997). Caring school communities. *Educational Psychology, 32*(3), 137–151.

Battistich, V., Solomon, D., Watson, M., Solomon, J., & Schaps, E. (1989). Effects of an elementary school program to enhance prosocial behaviors on children's cognitive-social problem solving skills and strategies. *Journal of Applied Developmental Psychology, 10*(2), 147–169.

Bell, A. J., Rosen, L. A., & Dynlacht, D. (1994). Truancy intervention. *The Journal of Research and Development in Education 57*(3), 203–211.

Bell, S. K., Coleman, J. K., Anderson, A., Whelan, J. P., & Wilder, C. (2000). The effectiveness of peer mediation in a low-SES rural elementary school. *Psychology in the Schools, 37,* 505–516.

Bernard, B. (1993). Fostering resiliency in kids. *Educational Leadership, 51*(3), 44–48.

Bodine, R., & Crawford, D. (1998). *The handbook of conflict resolution education.* San Francisco: Jossey-Bass.

Bodine, R., Crawford, D., & Schrumpf, F. (1994). *Creating the peaceable school: A comprehensive program for teaching conflict resolution.* Champaign, IL: Research Press.

Bosworth, K., Espelage, D., & Dubay, T. (1998). A computer-based violence prevention intervention for young adolescents: Pilot study. *Adolescence, 33*(132), 785–795.

Brinson Jr., K. H., Lovett, H. T., & Price, R. W. (2004). A matter of principle. *Journal of Cases in Educational Leadership, 7*(2).

Brison, J, Kottler, J, & Fisher, T. (2004). Cross-cultural conflict resolution in the schools: Some practical intervention strategies for counselors. *Journal of Counseling and Development, 82,* 294–301.

Brooks, B., & Kahn, M.. (1993). What makes character education programs work? *Educational Leadership, 51*(3), 19–21.

Burnstein, N. (1989). Preparing teachers to work with culturally diverse students: A teacher education model. *Journal of Teacher Education, 40*(5), 9–16.

Campbell, R. L., & Farrell, R. V. (1985). The identification of competencies for multicultural teacher education. *Negro Educational Review, 36*(3/4), 137–144.

Catalano, F. R., Arthur, M. W., Hawkins, J. D., Berglund, L., & Olson, J. J. (1998). Comprehensive community- and school-based interventions to prevent antisocial behavior. In R. Loeber & D. Farrington (Eds.), *Serious and violent juvenile offenders: Risk factors and successful interventions* (pp. 248–283). Thousand Oaks, CA: Sage.

CBS News (Producer). (1999, October). *CBS News "The early show" poll* [Computer file] (ICPSR02869-v1). New York: CBS News. (Ann Arbor, MI: Inter-university Consortium for Political and Social Research [Distributor])

Community Boards. (2008). *Peer mediation: Research & best practices.* Retrieved November 10, 2008, from http://www.communityboards.org

Cook, T. D., Murphy, R. F., & Hunt, D. H. (2000). Comer's school development program in Chicago: A theory-based evaluation. *American Educational Research Journal, 37*(2), 535–597.

Dahlen, E. R., & Deffenbacher, J. L. (2001). Anger management. In W. J. Lyddon & J. V. Jones Jr. (Eds.), *Empirically supported cognitive therapies: Current and future applications* (pp. 163–181). New York: Springer.

Davidman, L., & Davidman, P. (1994). *Teaching with a multicultural perspective: A practical guide.* New York: Longman.

DeBaryshe, B. D., & Fryxell, D. (1998). A developmental perspective on anger: Family and peer contexts. *Psychology in the Schools, 35,* 205–216.

Deutsch, M. (1993). Conflict resolution and cooperative learning in an alternative high school. *Cooperative Learning, 13*(4), 17–23.

Dryfoos, J. G. (1990). *Adolescents at risk: Prevalence and prevention.* New York: Oxford University Press.

Dwyer, K., Osher, D., & Warger, C. (1998). *Early warning, timely response: A guide to safe schools.* Washington, DC: U.S. Department of Education.

Elliott, D., & Mihalic, S. (2004). Issues in disseminating and replicating effective prevention programs. *Prevention Science, 5,* 47–53.

Enright, R. (1980). An integration of social cognitive development and cognitive processing: Educational applications. *American Educational Research Journal, 17*(1), 21–41.

Fisher, R., Ury, W., & Patton, B. (1991). *Getting to yes: Negotiating agreement without giving in.* New York: Penguin.

Flannery, D., Huff, C., & Manos, M. (1996). Youth gangs: A developmental perspective. In T. P. Gullotta, G. R. Adams, & R. Montemayor (Eds.), *Advances in adolescent development: Vol. 10. Delinquency, juvenile justice, and adolescence* (pp. 175–204). Thousand Oaks, CA: Sage.

Franzwa, F., & Lockhart, C. (1998). The social origins and maintenance of gender: Communication styles, personality types, and grid-group theory. *Sociological Perspectives, 41*(1), 185–208.

Gallup. (1999, August). Social and economic indicators: Education. Retrieved August 1999 from http://www.gallup.com

Gentry, D., & Benenson, W. (1993). School-to-home transfer of conflict management skills among school-age children. *Families in Society, 74*(2), 67–73.

Gerberding, J. L. (2005). *Press release: Dr. Gerberding's remarks at the National Press Club Conference; The state of the CDC—fiscal year 2004—protecting health for life.* Retrieved November 10, 2008, from http://www.cdc.gov/media/pressrel/r050222b.htm

Gilligan, C. (1982). *In a different voice.* Cambridge, MA: Harvard University Press.

Girard, K., & Koch, S. (1996). *Conflict resolution in the schools.* San Francisco: Jossey-Bass.

Gordon, T. (1979). Commentary. In R. Bolton (Author), *People skills: How to assert yourself, listen to others, and resolve conflicts* (pp. 3–7). New York: Simon & Schuster.

Gottfredson, D. C., & Gottfredson, G. D. (2002). Quality of school-based prevention programs: Results from a national survey. *Journal of Research in Crime and Delinquency, 39*, 3–35.

Grossman, D. C., Neckerman, H. J., Koepsell, T. D., Liu, P. Y., Asher, K. N., Beland, K., et al. (1997). Effectiveness of a violence prevention curriculum among children in elementary school. *Journal of the American Medical Association, 277*(20), 1605–1611.

Harter, S. (1990). Identity and self development. In S. Feldman and G. Elliott (Eds.), *At the threshold: The developing adolescent* (pp. 352–387). Cambridge, MA: Harvard University Press.

Hawkins, D. (1992). *Social development strategy: Building protective factors in your community.* Seattle, WA: Developmental Research.

Hoy, W., & Feldman, J. (1987). Organization health: The concept and its measure. *Journal of Research and Development in Education, 20*(4), 30–37.

Huizinga, D., Loeber, R. & Thornberry, T. P. (Eds.). (1995, July). *Recent findings from the Program of Research on the Causes and Correlates of Delinquency.* Washington, DC: U.S. Department of Justice, Office of Justice Programs, Office of Juvenile Justice and Delinquency Prevention.

Huesmann, L. R., Guerra, N. G., & Zelli, A. (1994). Normative orientation to beliefs about aggression scale (NOBAGS). Unpublished manuscript, University of Michigan Research Center for Group Dynamics, Institute for Social Research.

Infante, D., & Wigley, C. (1986). Verbal aggressiveness: An interpersonal model and measure. *Communication Monographs, 53*(1), 61–69.

Johnson, D. W., & Johnson, R. (1993). Cooperative learning and conflict resolution. *The Fourth R* (National Association for Mediation in Education), *42*(1), 2.

Johnson, D. W., & Johnson, R. (2001). Peer mediation in an inner-city school. *Urban Education, 36*(2), 165–179.

Johnson, D. W., Johnson, R., Dudley, B., & Burnett, R. (1992). Teaching students to be peer mediators. *Educational Leadership, 50*(1), 10–13.

Jones, E. M., Ryan, K. & Bohlin, K.. (1998). Character education and teacher education: How are prospective teachers being prepared to foster good character in students? *Action in Teacher Education, 20*(4), 11–28.

Jones, T. S. (2004). Conflict resolution education: The field, the findings, and the future. *Conflict Resolution Quarterly, 22*(1/2), 233–267.

Jordan, K. M., Vaughan, J. S., & Woodworth, K. J. (1997). I will survive: Lesbian, gay, and bisexual youths' experience of high school. *Journal of Gay and Lesbian Social Services, 7*(4), 17–33.

Kingberry Productions Inc. (2008). *Oh, my manners: A K–12 curriculum.* Bloomfield Hills, MI: Author.

Kingery, P. M., & Walker, H. M. (2002). What we know about school safety. In M. R. Shinn, H. M. Walker, & G. Stoner (Eds.), *Interventions for academic and behavior problems: Vol. 2. Preventive and remedial approaches* (pp. 71–88). Bethesda, MD: National Association of School Psychologists.

Kluckhohn, F. R., & Strondtbeck, F. (1961). *Variations in value orientations.* Evanston, IL: Row, Peterson.

Knoff, H., & Batsche, G. (1995). Project achieve: Analyzing a school reform process for at-risk and underachieving students. *School Psychology Review, 24*(4), 579–603.

Kohlberg, L. (1976). Moral stages and moralization: The cognitive-developmental approach. In T. Likona (Ed.), *Moral development and behavior: Theory, research and social issues* (pp. 31–53). New York: Holt, Rinehart, & Winston.

Kohlberg, L. (1984). *The psychology of moral development.* San Francisco: Harper-Row.

Kohn, A. (1997). The trouble with character education. In A. Molnar (Ed.), *The construction of children's character* (96th Yearbook of the National Society for the Study of Education: Part II; pp. 154–162). Chicago: University of Chicago Press.

Kowalski, R., & Limber, S. (2007). Electronic bullying among middle school students. *Journal of Adolescent Health, 41*(6), 22–30.

Kreidler, W. (1994). *Conflict resolution in the middle school.* Cambridge, MA: Educators for Social Responsibility.

Lang, M., & Salas, G. (1998). Multicultural education in Michigan's public schools: Policy and practice. *Equity & Excellence in Education, 31*(3), 64–72.

Lantieri, L., & Patti, J. (1996). *Waging peace in our schools.* Boston: Beacon Press.

Levy, J. (1989). Conflict resolution in elementary and secondary education. *Mediation Quarterly, 7*(1), 73–87.

Likona, T. (1991). *Educating for character: How our schools can teach respect and responsibility.* New York: Bantam Books.

Lockwood, A. T. (1999). Newsletter of the comprehensive center region VI. *School Safety, 4*(1), 2–3.

Mabie, Grant E. (2003). Making schools safe for the 21st century: An interview with Ronald D. Stephens. *The Educational Forum, 67*(7), 156–162. Retrieved November 10, 2008, from http://findarticles.com/p/articles/mi_qa4013/is_/ai_n9216003

Marsh, D., Serafica, F., & Barenboim, C. (1981). Interrelationships among perspective taking, interpersonal problem solving, and interpersonal understanding. *Journal of Genetic Psychology, 138,* 37–48.

Marzano, R. (1992). *A different kind of classroom: Teaching with dimensions of learning.* Alexandria, VA: Association for Supervision and Curriculum Development.

Maslow, A. (1968). *Toward a psychology of being.* New York: Van Nostrand Reinhold.

Maxfield, M. G. (2001). *Guide to frugal evaluation for criminal justice.* Washington, DC: National Institute of Justice.

Maxwell, J. (1989). Mediation in the schools: Self-regulation, self-esteem, and self-discipline. *Mediation Quarterly, 7*(2), 149–155.

Mihalic, S. (2004). The importance of implementation fidelity. *Emotional & Behavioral Disorders in Youth, 4,* 83–105.

Mihalic, S., & Aultman-Bettridge, T. (2004). A guide to effective school-based prevention programs: Environmentally focused programs. In William L. Turk (ed.), *School crime and policing* (pp. 246–262). Upper Saddle River, NJ: Prentice Hall.

Milstein, R. L., & Wetterhall, S. F. (1999). Framework for program evaluation in public health. *Morbidity and Mortality Weekly Report, 48*(RR-11), 1–40.

Narvaez, D., Bentley, J., Gleason, T., & Samuels, J. (1998). Moral theme comprehension in third graders, fifth graders, and college students. *Reading Psychology, 19*(2), 217–241.

National Center for Education Statistics. (2007). *Digest of education statistics, 2006* (NCES 2007-017). Washington, DC: U.S. Department of Education.

National Center for Education Statistics (NCES) and Bureau of Justice Statistics (BJS). (2005). *School crime supplement (SCS).* Washington, DC: U.S. Department of Education.

National i-SAFE Survey. (2004). *National i-SAFE survey finds over half of students are being harassed online.* Retrieved July 21, 2004, from www.isafe.com.

National Resource Center for Youth Mediation. (1995). *Student mediation in elementary schools.* Albuquerque: The New Mexico Center for Dispute Resolution.

Neckerman, H., Asher, K. & Pavlidis, K. (1994). *Social interaction observation system.* Unpublished manuscript. Harborview Injury Prevention and Research Center, Seattle, WA.

Noddings, N. (1988, December 7). Schools face crisis in caring. *Education Week,* p. 32.

Nucci, L. (1989). *Moral development and character education: A dialogue.* Berkeley, CA: McCutchan.

O'Conor, A. (1994). Who gets called queer in school? Lesbian, gay, and bisexual teenagers, homophobia, and high school. *The High School Journal, 77*(1/2), 7–12.

Ohio Commission on Dispute Resolution and Conflict Management. (1999). *Annual report of the Ohio Commission on Dispute Resolution and Conflict Management.* Columbus, OH: Author.

Pate, G. (1988). Research on reducing prejudice. *Social Education, 52*(4), 287–289.

Patterson, G. (1982). *Coercive family process.* Eugene, OR: Castalia.

Phillips, D. A. (2007). Punking and bullying: Strategies in middle school, high school, and beyond. *Journal of Interpersonal Violence, 22*(2), 158–178.

Piaget, J. (1932). *The moral judgment of the child.* New York: Free Press.

Powell, K. E., Muir-McClain, L., & Halasyamani, L. (1995). A review of selected school-based conflict resolution and peer mediation projects. *Journal of School Health, 65*(10), 426–431.

Power, C., Higgins, A., & Kohlberg, L. (1989). The habit of the common life: Building character through democratic community schools. In L. Nucci (Ed.), *Moral development and character education: A dialogue* (pp. 125–143). Berkeley, CA: McCutchan.

Pritchard, I. (1998). *Moral education and character* (Report No. OR-88-505). Washington, DC: Department of Education, Office of Research. (ERIC Document Reproduction Service No. ED304390)

Quinn, M. M., Osher, D., Hoffman, C. C., & Hanley, T. V. (1998). *Safe, drug-free, and effective schools for ALL students: What works!* Washington, DC: Center for Effective Collaboration and Practice, American Institute for Research.

Rahim, M., Buntzman, G., & White, D.. (1999). An empirical study of the stages of moral development and conflict management styles. *International Journal of Conflict Management, 10*(2), 154–171.

Resnick, M. D., Bearman, P. S., Blum, R. W., Bauman, K. E., Harris, K. M., Jones, J., et al. (1997). Protecting adolescents from harm: Findings from the National Longitudinal Study on adolescent health. *Journal of the American Medical Association, 278*(10), 823–832.

Robarchek, C. A. (1997). A community of interests: Semai conflict resolution. In D. P. Fry & K. Björkqvist (Eds.), *Cultural variation in conflict resolution: Alternatives to violence* (pp. 51–58). Mahwah, NJ: Lawrence Erlbaum.

Robelen, E. W. (2003, September 24). States report few schools as dangerous. *Education Week, 23,* 1–3.

Robins, L. N., & Ratcliff, K. S. (1978). *Long-range outcomes associated with school truancy.* Washington, DC: Public Health Service.

Rogers, M., Miller, N., & Hennigan, K. (1981). Cooperative games as an intervention to promote cross-racial acceptance. *American Educational Research Journal, 18*(4), 513–516.

Rohrman, D. (1993). Combating truancy in our schools: A community effort. *NASSP Bulletin, 76*(549), 40–45.

Rossi, P., Freeman, H., & Lipseg, M. (1999). *Evaluation: A systematic approach.* Thousand Oaks, CA: Sage.

Rutter, M., Maughan, B., Mortimore, P., Ouston, J., & Smith, A. (1979). *Fifteen thousand hours.* Cambridge, MA: Harvard University.

Ryan, K. (1989). In defense of character education. In L. Nucci (Ed.), *Moral development and character education: A dialogue* (pp. 3–17). Berkeley, CA: McCutchan.

Ryan, K., & Bohlin, K. (1999). *Building character in schools: Practical ways to bring moral instruction to life.* San Francisco: Jossey-Bass.

Sadalla, G., Henriquez, M., & Holmberg, M. (1987). *Conflict resolution: A secondary school curriculum.* San Francisco: Community Board Program.

San Francisco Community Board Program. (1992). *Starting a conflict managers program: Self-report.* San Francisco: Author.

Schneider, T., Walker, H. M., & Sprague, J. R. (2000). *Safe school design: A handbook for educational leaders.* Eugene, OR: ERIC Clearinghouse on Educational Management.

Schrumpf, F., Crawford, D., & Usafel, H. (1991). *Peer mediation: Conflict resolution in the school program guide.* Champaign, IL: Research Press.

Scieszka, J. (1989). *True story of the three little pigs by A. Wolf.* New York: Putnam Books.

Secor, D. (1997). *Development and validation of the children's constructive conflict resolution scale.* Unpublished doctoral dissertation, Temple University, Philadelphia.

Selman, R. (1980). *The growth of interpersonal understanding: Developmental and clinical analyses.* San Diego, CA: Academic Press.

Selman, R. (1981). The development of interpersonal competence: The role of understanding in conduct. *Developmental Review, 1,* 401–422.

Selman, R., Jaquette, D., & Bruss-Saunders, E. (1979). *Assessing interpersonal understanding: An interview and scoring manual.* Cambridge, MA: Harvard-Judge Baker Social Reasoning Project.

Sheldon, S., & Epstein, J. (2002). Improving student behavior and school discipline with family and community involvement. *Education and Urban Society, 35*(1), 4–26.

Simpson, E. (1989). *Good lives and moral education.* New York: Peter Lang.

Skinner, B. F. (1974). *About behaviorism.* New York: Vintage Books.

Snyder, H. N., & Sickmund, M. (1995). *Juvenile offenders and victims: A national report.* Washington, DC: U.S. Department of Justice, Office of Justice Programs, Office of Juvenile Justice and Delinquency Prevention.

Snyder, H. N., & Sickmund, M. (1999). *Juvenile offenders and victims: 1999 national report.* Washington, DC: Office of Juvenile Justice and Delinquency.

Solomon, D., Watson, M., Battistich, V., Schaps, E., & Delucchi, K. (1996). Creating classrooms that students experience as communities. *American Journal of Community Psychology, 24*(6), 719–748.

Solomon, D., Watson, M., Delucchi, K., Schaps, E., & Battistich, V. (1988). Enhancing children's prosocial behavior in the classroom. *American Educational Research Journal, 25*(4), 527–554.

Sprague, J., & Walker, H. (2000). Early identification and intervention for youth with antisocial and violent behavior. *Exceptional Children, 66*(3), 367–379.

Sprague, J. R., & Walker, H. M. (2005). *Safe and healthy schools: Practical prevention strategies.* New York: Guilford Press.

Stephens, R. (1995). *Safe schools: A handbook for violence prevention.* Bloomington, IN: National Educational Service.

Stevahn, L., Johnson, D., Johnson, R., Laginski, A. M., & O'Coin, I. (1996). Effects on high school students of integrating conflict resolution and peer mediation training into an academic unit. *Mediation Quarterly, 14*(1), 21–36.

Stomfay-Stitz, A. M. (1994). Conflict resolution and peer mediation: Pathways to safer schools. *Childhood Education, 70,* 279–282.

Studer, J. R. (2000). What the resilient child can teach us about reducing violence. *Reaching Today's Youth: The Community Circle of Caring Journal 4*(2), pp. 72–76.

Sweeney, B., & Carruthers, W. (1996). Conflict resolution: History, philosophy, theory, and education applications. *School Counselor, 43,* 326–344.

Theberge, S. & Karan, O. C. (2004). Six factors inhibiting the use of peer mediation in a junior high school. *Professional School Counseling, 7*(4), 283–290.

Thornton, L. (1997). [Multicultural/special education in the U.S. classroom]. Unpublished class material, University of Michigan–Dearborn, School of Education.

Toppo, G., & Schouten, F. (2003, September 19). School safety law benefits few students; 52 schools fit "dangerous" definitions. *USA Today,* p. A3.

U.S. Department of Education. (1998). *Annual report on school safety.* Washington, DC: U.S. Department of Education.

van de Vall, M., & C. Bolas. (1981, June). External vs. internal social policy researchers. *Knowledge: Creation, Diffusion, Utilization, 2,* 461–481.

Vygotsky, L. (1987). *The collected works of L. S. Vygotsky: Vol. 1. Problems of general psychology.* R. Riber & A. Corton (Eds.). New York: Plenum Press.

Walsh, D. (1988). Critical thinking to reduce prejudice. *Social Education, 52*(4), 280–282.

Warring, D., Johnson, D. W., Maruyama, G., & Johnson, R. (1985). Impact on different types of cooperative learning on cross-ethnic and cross-sex relationships. *Journal of Educational Psychology, 77*(1), 53–59.

Werner, E., & Smith, R. (1989). *Vulnerable but invincible: A longitudinal study of resilient children and youth.* New York: Adams, Bannister, and Cox.

Wynne, E., & Wahlberg, H. (Eds). (1984). *Developing character: Transmitting knowledge.* Posen, IL: ARL.

Wynne, E., & Wahlberg, H. (1985). The complementary goals of character development and academic excellence. *Educational Leadership, 43*(4), 15–18.

Zuckerman, B., Augustyn, M., Groves, B., & Parker, S. (1995). Silent victims revisited: The special case of domestic violence. *Pediatrics, 96*(3), 511–513.

Index

Academic performance, 15–16
  character education, 54
  peer mediation, 97
Academic standards, 9, 10
Access control, 38, 40–41
Achenbach Child Behavior Checklist
  (CBCL), 141–142
Achenbach Teacher Report Form (TRF),
  141–142
Active listening skills:
  clarification, 75 (figure), 76
  conflict resolution education, 70–71,
    74–77, 84, 85, 121
  diversity education, 121
  encouragement, 75 (figure), 76
  paraphrasing, 75
  reflection, 75 (figure), 76
  summarizing, 75 (figure), 76–77
  validation, 75 (figure), 76
Active listening vocabulary, 70–71, 74–75
Adult model facilitation, 93
Africa, 125
African-American students,
  2, 26, 128 (figure)
Aggressive behavior, 123, 135–136,
  138–139, 141, 142
Alcohol use, 16
American Bar Association, 111–112
American Institute for Research, 38,
  39–40 (figure)
Anger management, 69–70, 89
Antibias education, 126–127
Arab-American students, 26, 128 (figure)
Art, 85–86
Asian-American students, 26, 128 (figure)
Assertiveness:
  conflict resolution education, 78–79
  defined, 78

  student exercise, 79
  student training, 78–79
Attitudes:
  conflict resolution education,
    27–28, 36–37 (figure)
  peer mediation, 109–110
  school safety program evaluation, 139,
    140 (figure), 141
Authoritarian teaching style, 27–28, 63, 121

Behaviorism, 53, 80
Belief systems, 118–120
Biased-based violence, 9, 10, 121–122
Boston Plan of Excellence in the Public
  Schools, 89
Bullying behaviors, 9, 10, 15, 16
  case study, 28, 112–113
  cyberbullying, 122
  peer mediation, 112–113
Business community activities, 11

California Child Development
  Project, 60–61, 65
Case study:
  bullying behaviors, 28, 112–113
  cliques, 29
  cultural diversity, 26
  environmental safety, 31
  peer mediation, 112–113
  school safety assessment, 26, 28, 29, 30, 31
  student profiling, 30
Center for Peace and Conflict Studies,
  Wayne State University, 3
Centers for Disease Control and
  Prevention, 133
Character education:
  academic performance, 54
  action opportunities, 64

169

CORWIN
A SAGE Company

The Corwin logo—a raven striding across an open book—represents the union of courage and learning. Corwin is committed to improving education for all learners by publishing books and other professional development resources for those serving the field of PreK–12 education. By providing practical, hands-on materials, Corwin continues to carry out the promise of its motto: **"Helping Educators Do Their Work Better."**